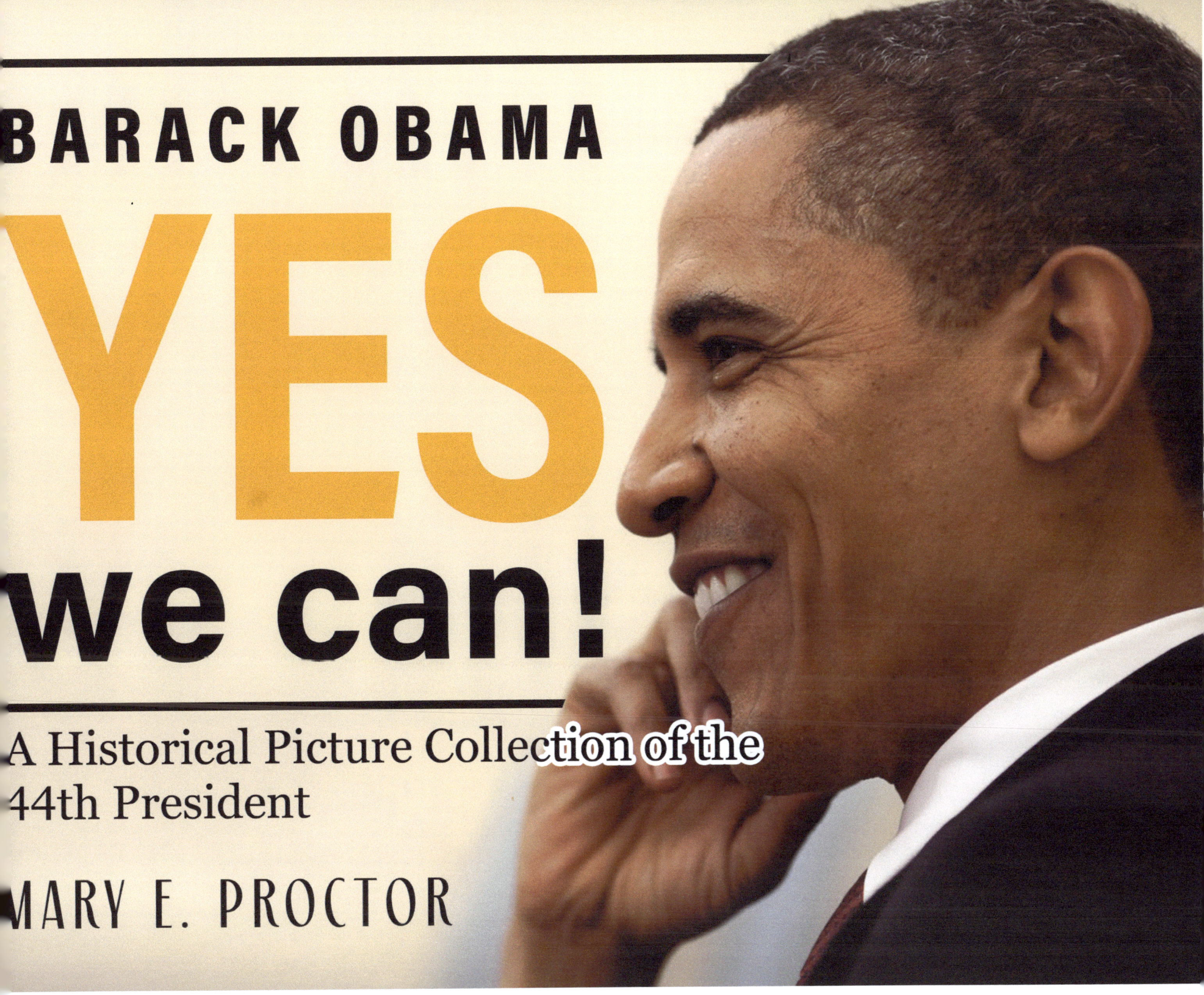

BARACK OBAMA

YES
we can!

A Historical Picture Collection of the 44th President

MARY E. PROCTOR

This publication contains the opinions and ideas of its author. It is intended to provide helpful and informative material on the subjects addressed in the publication. The author and publisher specifically disclaim all responsibility for any liability, loss or risk, personal or otherwise, which is incurred as a consequence, directly or indirectly, of the use and application of any of the contents of this book.

WORKBOOK PRESS LLC
187 E Warm Springs Rd,
Suite B285, Las Vegas, NV 89119, USA

Website: https://workbookpress.com/
Hotline: 1-888-818-4856
Email: admin@workbookpress.com

Ordering Information:
Quantity sales. Special discounts are available on quantity purchases by corporations, associations, and others. For details, contact the publisher at the address above.

Library of Congress Control Number:
ISBN-13:   978-1-958176-30-6 (Paperback Version)
              978-1-958176-31-3 (Digital Version)

REV. DATE: 05/11/2022

Certificate of Registration

This Certificate issued under the seal of the Copyright Office in accordance with title 17, *United States Code*, attests that registration has been made for the work identified below. The information on this certificate has been made a part of the Copyright Office records.

Kay H. Tingle

Acting United States Register of Copyrights and Director

Registration Number

VAu 1-321-091

Effective Date of Registration:
March 21, 2017

Title *Historical Picture Collection of the 44th President*

Title of Work:	Historical Picture Collection of the 44th President
Previous or Alternate Title:	Barback Obama - Yes We Can - A Historical Picture Collection of the 44th President
Nature of Claim:	Photographs

Completion/Publication

Year of Completion: 2016

Author *Mary E. Proctor*

• **Author:**	Mary E. Proctor
Author Created:	compilation of text and photographs
Year Born:	1943

Copyright Claimant *Mary E. Proctor*

Copyright Claimant:	Mary E. Proctor
	2404 Berkley St., Temple Hills, MD, 20748

Limitation of copyright claim

Material excluded from this claim:	pre-existing material from other sources
Previously registered:	No
New material included in claim:	compilation of text and photographs

Certification *Mary E. Proctor*

Name:	Mary E. Proctor
Date:	June 28, 2018

Correspondence: Yes

THE DUNHAMS

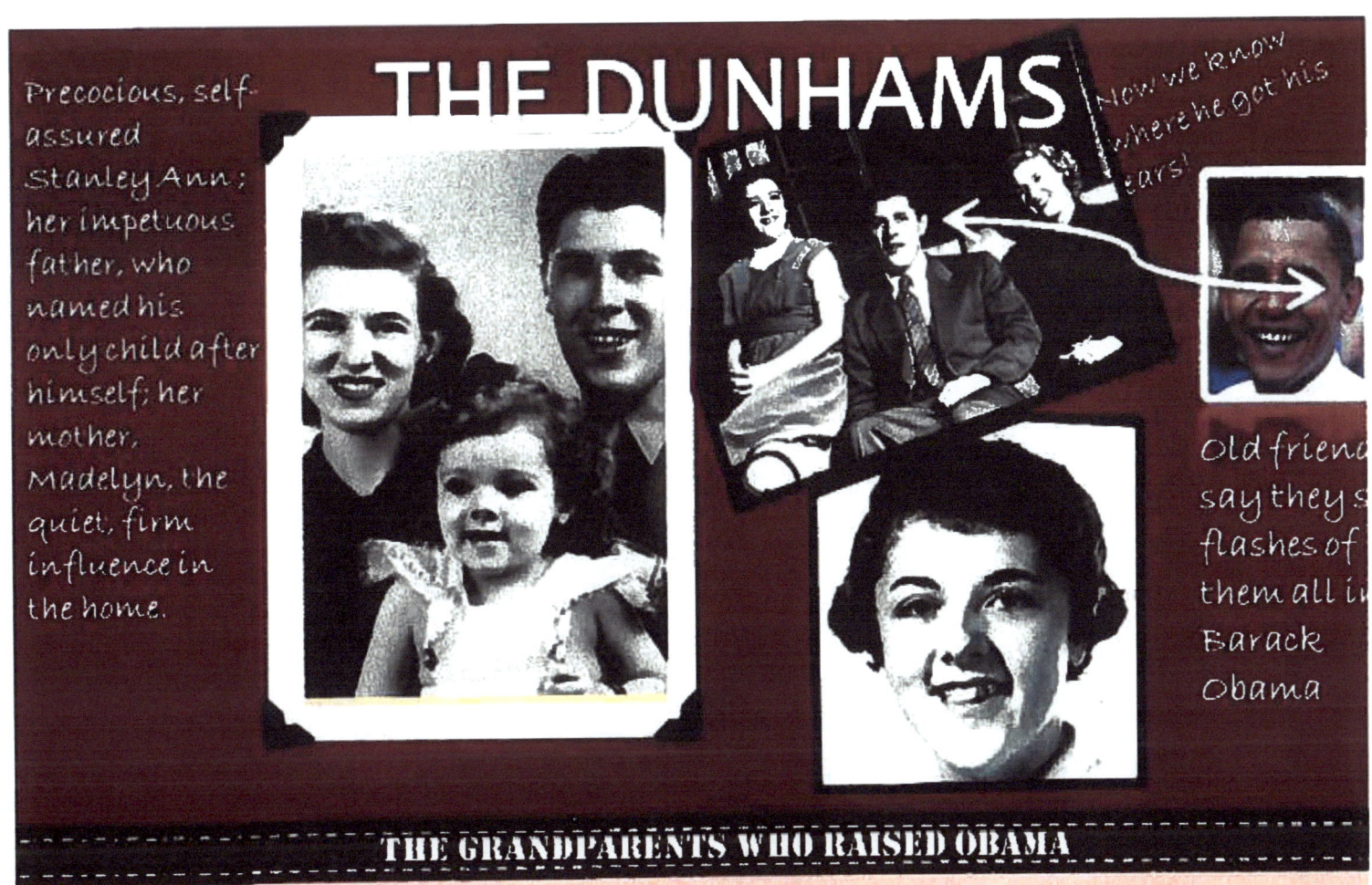

Precocious, self-assured Stanley Ann; her impetuous father, who named his only child after himself; her mother, Madelyn, the quiet, firm influence in the home.

Now we know where he got his ears!

Old friend[s] say they s[ee] flashes of them all i[n] Barack Obama

THE GRANDPARENTS WHO RAISED OBAMA

Madelyn Dunham, Obama's grandmother, blazed a feminist trail in Hawaii banking circles in the late 1960s and early 1970s and rose to become one of the Bank of Hawaii's first female vice presidents.

In 1817, Obama's great-grandfather Rolla Payne registered for the WWI draft. This 24-year-old bookkeeper worked for an oil well supply company in Tulsa, Oklahoma and would be called up to serve in the First World War. (Another great-grandfather and a great-great-grandfather also registered for the draft, although neither served in the Great War.)

Obama's great-great-grandfather Robert Wolfley served in the Ohio Infantry during the Civil War. This Union soldier kept the rank of private throughout his service.

http://obamascrapbook.com

In January 1942, Illinois Sen. Barack Obama's 24-year-old grandfather, Stanley Dunham, said goodbye to his wife and infant and enlisted in the U.S. Army. "He signed up for duty, joined Patton's army and marched across Europe," said Sen. Obama of his grandfather's service.

Proud

To Be

American

4

MERCER ISLAND IS A 5-MILE-LONG STRETCH OF DOUGLAS FIRS AND CEDARS, JUST ACROSS FROM SEATTLE IN LAKE WASHINGTON

Barack Obama's mother was described as a "strong-willed, unconventional member of the Mercer Island High School graduating class of 1960."

After she graduated, her family moved to Hawaii, where she attended the University of Hawaii

DEBATE TEAM

Barack Obama was born in Honolulu, Hawaii on August 4, 1961, to Barack Obama, Sr. and Ann Dunham (born in Wichita, Kansas). His parents met while both were attending the University of Hawaii at Manoa, where his father was enrolled as a foreign student.

Barack

http://obamascrapbook.com

6

Barack

Barack
Obama plays
on the beach
with his
grandfather
on his
mother's side,
Stanley
Armour
Dunham

Birth

Granddad

7

A young Barack Obama plays in the Hawaiian surf

Barack

http://obamascrapbook.com

Birth

Granddad

Play

8

Barack Obama rides a tricycle during his childhood in Hawaii

Birth

Granddad

Play

Toys

Barack
http://obamascrapbook.com

9

This 1960's photo shows Barack with his baseball bat in Hawaii

Barack

Birth

Granddad

Play

Toys

Sports

10

When he was six, Obama's mother remarried, and the family moved to Indonesia

His mother got him up at 4:30 to give him English lessons before he went to school and she went to work

Ann Dunham, at home in Jakarta, with her second husband, Lolo Soetoro (who worked for Shell Oil), their daughter Maya, and Barack

BARACK ATTENDED A CATHOLIC SCHOOL IN JAKARTA FOR TWO YEARS, THEN, WHEN THE FAMILY MOVED, TRANSFERRED INTO A PUBLIC SCHOOL CLOSER TO HOME FOR THE NEXT TWO YEARS

http://obamascrapbook.com

11

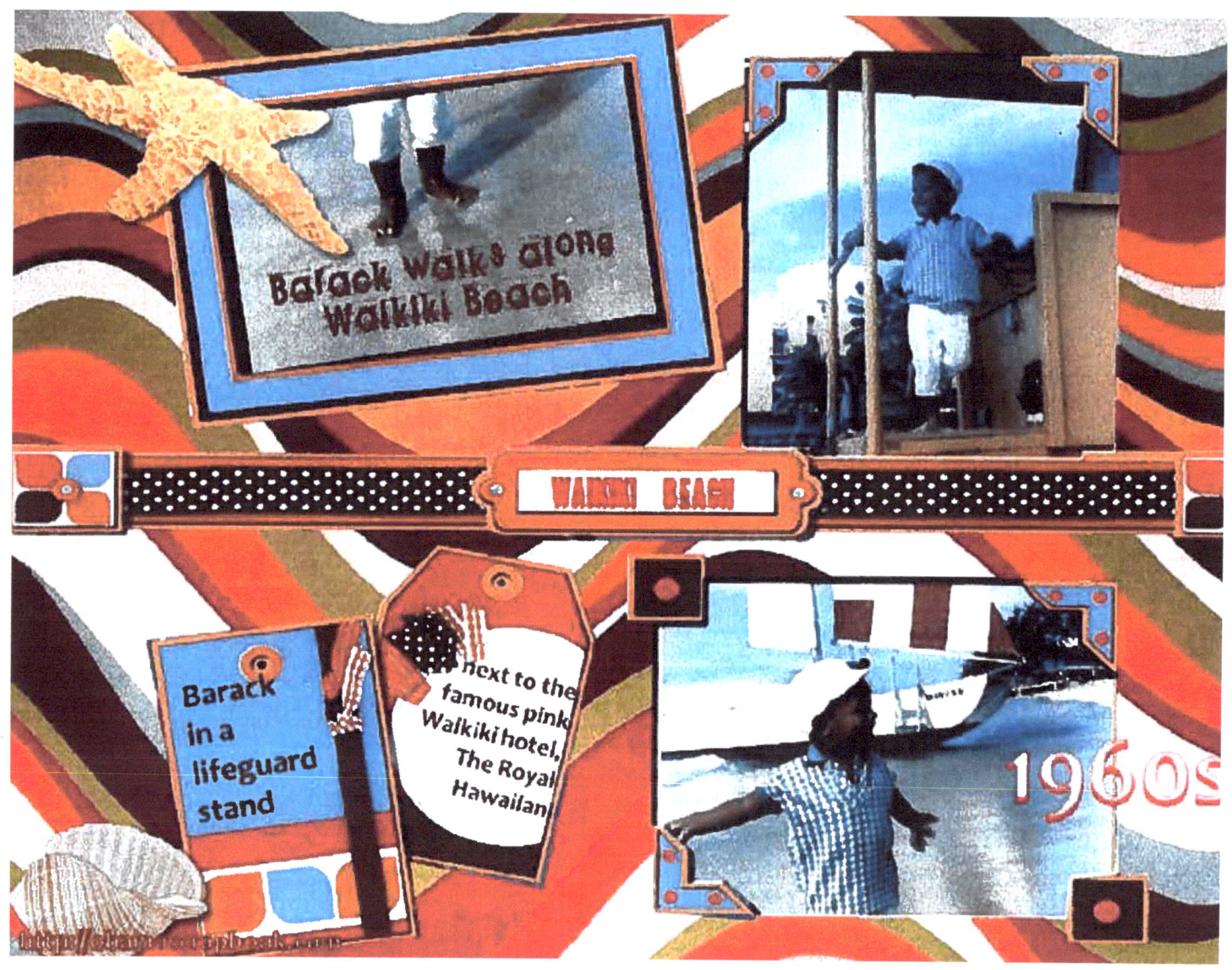

Barack walks along
Waikiki Beach

WAIKIKI BEACH

Barack
in a
lifeguard
stand

next to the
famous pink
Waikiki hotel,
The Royal
Hawaiian

1960S

12

1970s

EVEN IN INDONESIA, HE USED TO TELL HIS MOM THAT HE WANTED TO BE PRESIDENT OF THE UNITED STATES SOMEDAY

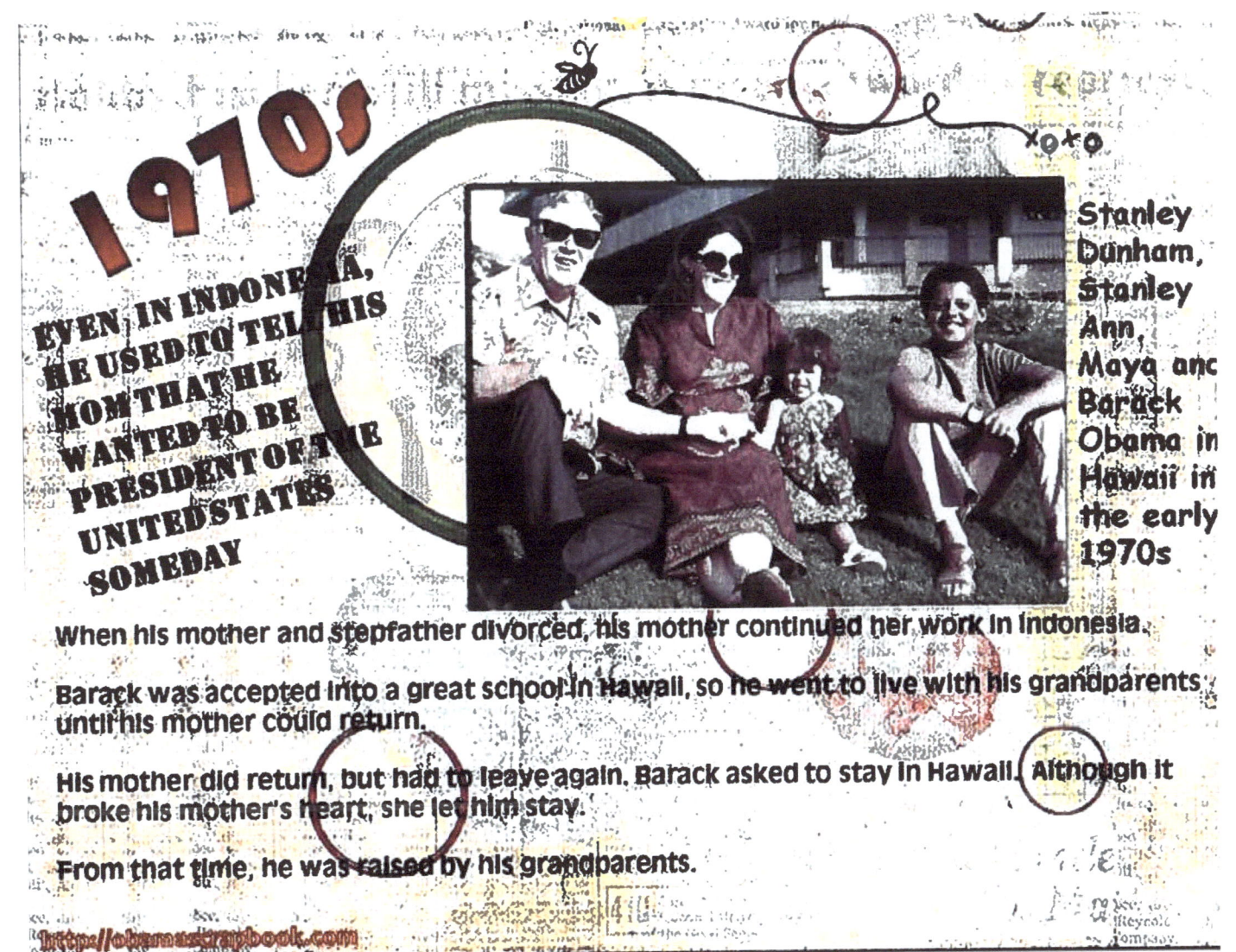

Stanley Dunham, Stanley Ann, Maya and Barack Obama in Hawaii in the early 1970s

When his mother and stepfather divorced, his mother continued her work in Indonesia.

Barack was accepted into a great school in Hawaii, so he went to live with his grandparents until his mother could return.

His mother did return, but had to leave again. Barack asked to stay in Hawaii. Although it broke his mother's heart, she let him stay.

From that time, he was raised by his grandparents.

13

School in Hawaii

1972

Founded in 1841, Punahou School was designed originally to provide a quality education to the children of Congregational missionaries

http://obamascrapbook.com

14

DAD

Barack Obama Sr. poses with his son in the Honolulu airport during Obama Sr.'s only visit to see his son while he was growing up in Hawaii. Young Barack was in the 5th grade when the photo was taken.

Barack Obama Sr., a native of Kenya, met his futu... wife while they were students at the Universlty... Hawaii. In 1963, he left his family to continue his stud... at Harva...

CHRISTMAS

Barack aged about 10, with hi mother and his father, who brie visited them to celebrate Christmas in Hawaii

I'll be home for *Christmas*

16

1970s

Barack with
Mom, Maya
and Granddad
in Hawaii

17

Punahou School

Honolulu, Hawaii

1977

The JV team at Punahou School, Hawaii

18

PUNAHOU SCHOOL IS NONSECTARIAN BUT RETAINS ITS CHRISTIAN HERITAGE

Barack Obama, in front row, fourth from right, posing with his ninth-grade homeroom class outside Punahou School, which is the largest private independent school west of the Mississippi

Ninth Grade

1976

High school senior Obama takes a shot during a basketball game with his team from the Punahou School in 1979

At his high school graduation, Barack Obama gets a hug from his grandmother Madelyn, as his grandfather bear

SISTER

THE UNIVERSITY of HAWAI'I

Barack hugs Maya at his high school graduation

Maya Soetoro-Ng, Barack Obama's half sister, teaches Education in American Society class at University of Hawaii. She poses here with her husband, Konrad Ng, and their daughter, Suhaila

21

BARACK OBAMA GRADUATING FROM PUNAHOU HIGH SCHOOL

1979

Obama accepting his high school diploma from the president of Punahou School, Dr. Roderick McPhee

Obama in New York City during the 1980s while a student at Columbia University. Obama received his B.A. degree in political science in 1983 from Columbia.

Columbia

Obama receives a visit from his grandparents, Stanley and Madelyn Dunham, in New York, 1982

23

1987

Obama traveled to Kenya in 1987 for a month-long visit to his father's family, then traveled back to Boston to begin law school at Harvard

24

RIP 1982

Obama's father's grave in Kisumu

Barack senior died in a road crash in in 1982, five years before his son paid his first visit to Kenya

BARACK OBAMA

Dreams from My Father

ETHIOPIA

KENYA

Nairobi

25

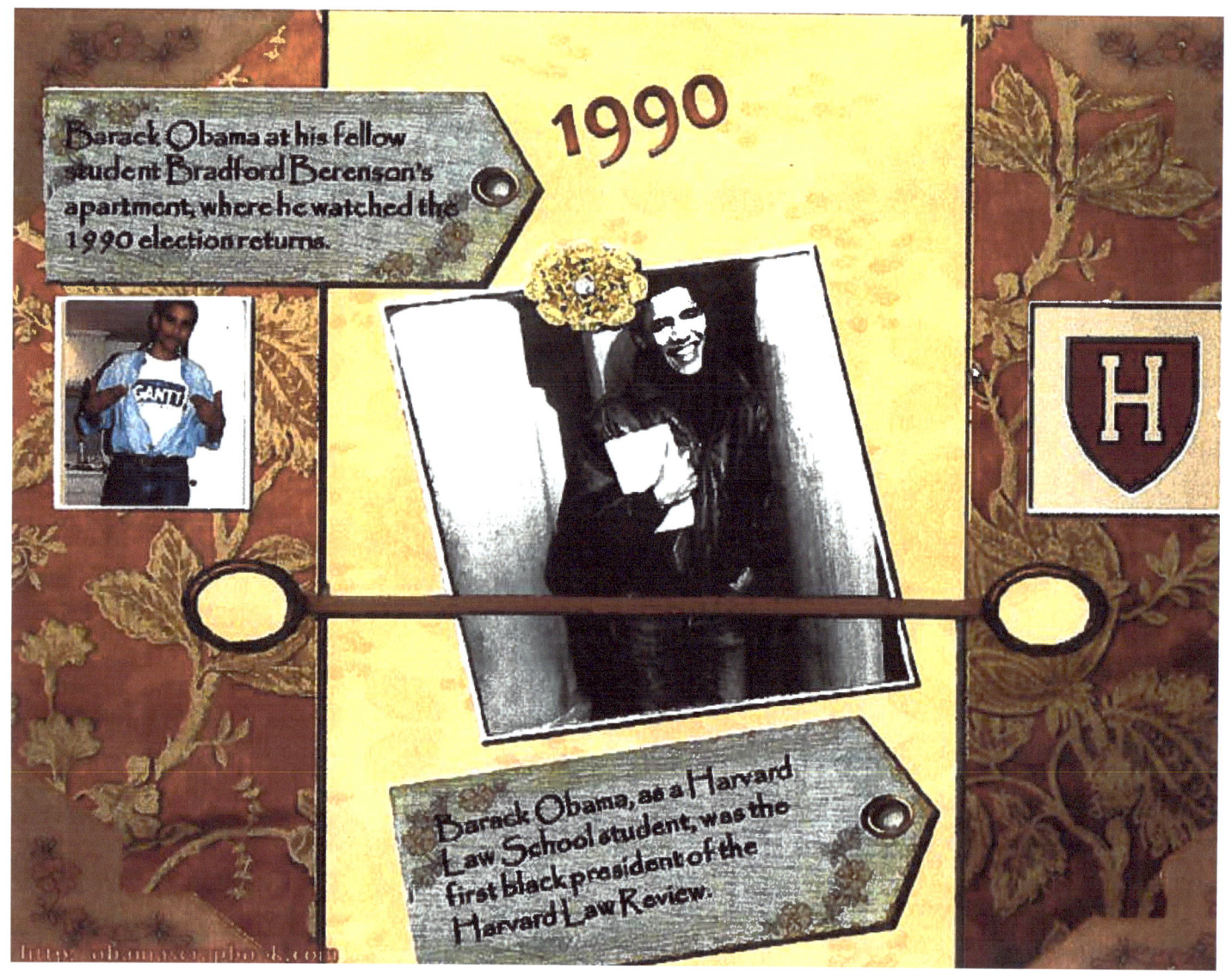

1990

Barack Obama at his fellow student Bradford Berenson's apartment, where he watched the 1990 election returns.

Barack Obama, as a Harvard Law School student, was the first black president of the Harvard Law Review.

H

1990

natural leader   impressive student   nice guy

celebrate
Life's
moments

Barack
Obama in
1990, when
he led the
Harvard Law
Review, the
most
powerful
legal journal
in the country

http://obamascrapbook.com

In Chicago, a young girl grew into a remarkable woman . . . .

Michelle Obama's childhood home in Chicago

"Michelle was from a middle-class family. They had a nice home. It wasn't a mansion, but it was just fine. It was a decent neighborhood."

The Robinsons grew up on the upper floor of a house built in the Twenties

Home

Michelle

Family

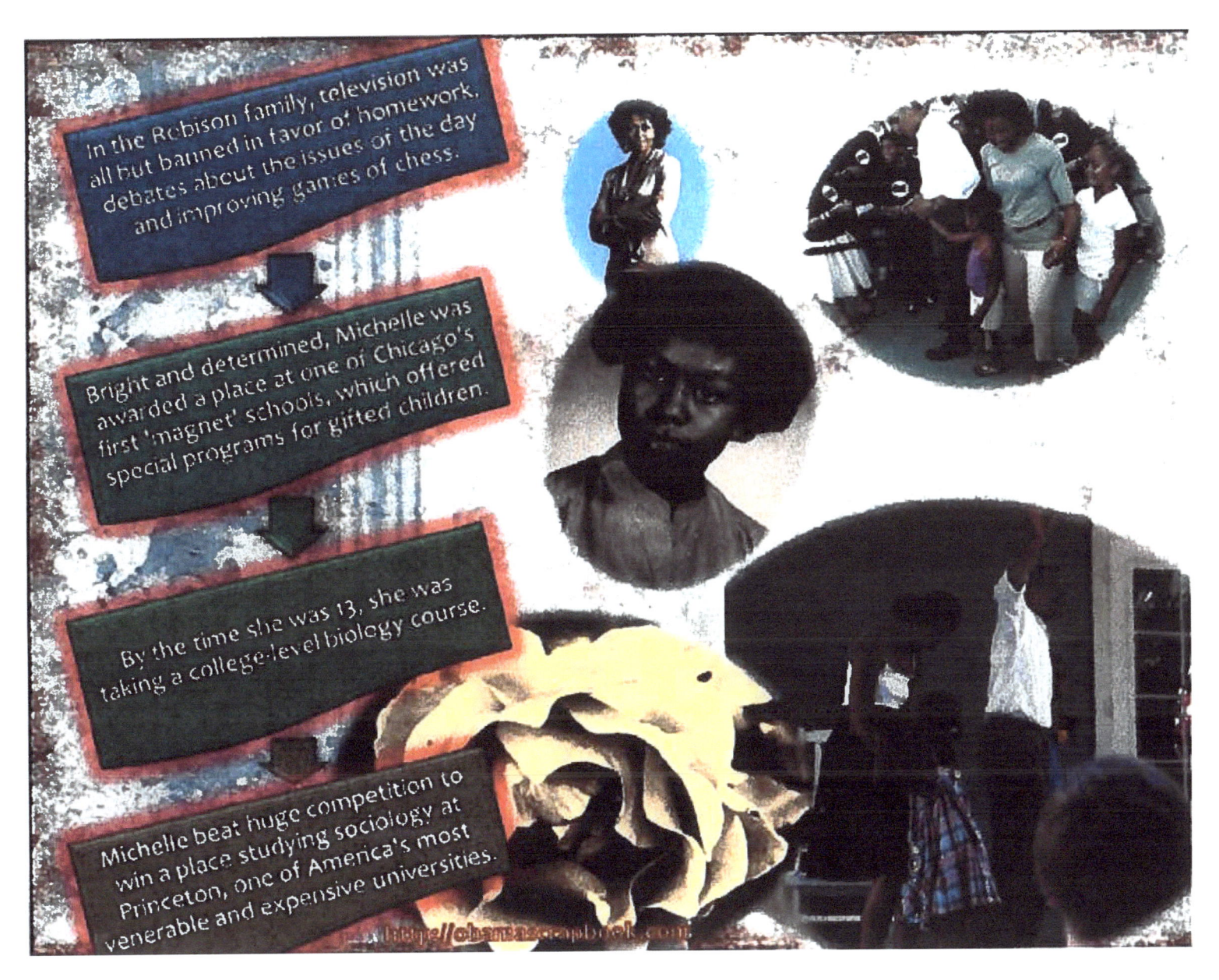

In the Robison family, television was all but banned in favor of homework, debates about the issues of the day and improving games of chess.

Bright and determined, Michelle was awarded a place at one of Chicago's first 'magnet' schools, which offered special programs for gifted children.

By the time she was 13, she was taking a college-level biology course.

Michelle beat huge competition to win a place studying sociology at Princeton, one of America's most venerable and expensive universities.

29

A Young Barack Obama

In 1989, Michelle was working at a downtown law firm and was assigned as advisor to a summer associate from Harvard

Although h reportedl didn't hav much interest i corporate law, he di have a lo of interes in Michel

After refusing to go out with him for a month, she agreed to go to dinner and then to a movie, *Do the Right Thing* on their first date

clinton sparks

KARDINAL OFFISHALL

DO THE RIGHT THING

GET FAMILIAR

SAL

Barack and Michelle
on their wedding day
Oct. 18, 1992, in
Chicago, Illinois

https://obamascrapbook.com

1992

Love

RIP·1995

Barack's mother, Ann's most lasting professional legacy was working with Indonesia's oldest bank to build the microfinance program in Indonesia and making the practice of granting tiny loans to credit-poor entrepreneurs a success.

ANN

Ann died in 1995 of cancer

MY MOM

http://obamascrapbook.com

34

2 0 0 7

Obama'08
BarackObama.com

spirit

A proud Maya campaigning for her brother

35

MALIA ANN WAS BORN IN 1998

Stanley Dunham, Obama's grandfather, who raised him, died in 1992

MEMORIES
fami

RIP 1992

http://obamascrapbook.com

Natasha (known as Sasha) was born in 2001

38

2004

2004

Palm Sunday Mass at St. Sabina's Church where Archbishop Desmond Tutu was speaking to the congregation April 4, 2004 in Chicago

http://obamascrapbook.com

39

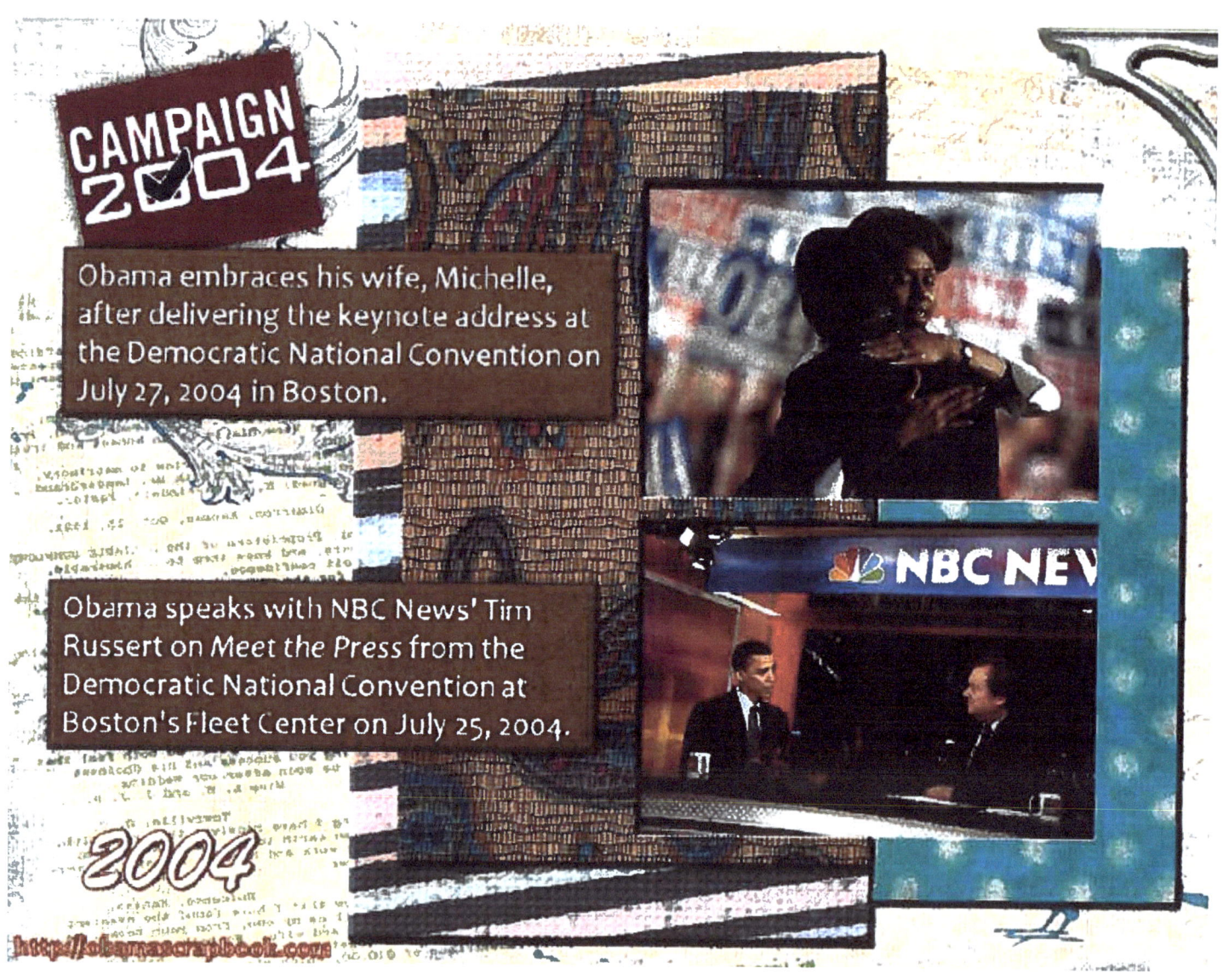

CAMPAIGN 2004

Obama embraces his wife, Michelle, after delivering the keynote address at the Democratic National Convention on July 27, 2004 in Boston.

Obama speaks with NBC News' Tim Russert on *Meet the Press* from the Democratic National Convention at Boston's Fleet Center on July 25, 2004.

2004

http://obamascrapbook.com

Yes, it is the Bible

2005

Obama with his wife, Michelle, Vice President Dick Cheney, and daughters Malia and Sasha during the reenactment of a swearing-in ceremony on Capitol Hill on January 4, 2005 in Washington, DC

Bono and Obama talk at the National Prayer Breakfast in Washington, DC

http://obamascrapbook.com

41

Democratic State Sen. Barack Obama trounced Republican candidate Alan Keyes in the contest to become the United States' only black senator

2004

Obama celebrates his forty-third birthday with his family during a fundraiser on August 4, 2004 in Matteson, Illinois.

Obama awaits election returns with his wife and daughters on November 2, 2004 in Chicago.

Senator Joseph Biden and Senator Obama confide during a Senate Foreign Relations Committee hearing on Capitol Hill on April 11, 2005 in Washington, DC.

OBAMA THROWS THE OPENING BA[LL]
AT GAME TWO OF THE AMERICAN
LEAGUE CHAMPIONSHIP SERIES
BETWEEN THE LOS ANGELES
ANGELS AND CHICAGO WHITE SOX
ON OCTOBER 12, 2005 AT U.S.
CELLULAR FIELD IN CHICAGO.

Obama tours New
Orleans' heavily
damaged Lakeview
neighborhood July 21,
2006 after Hurricane
Katrina.

2006

44

Once upon a time

2005

http://obamascrapbook.com

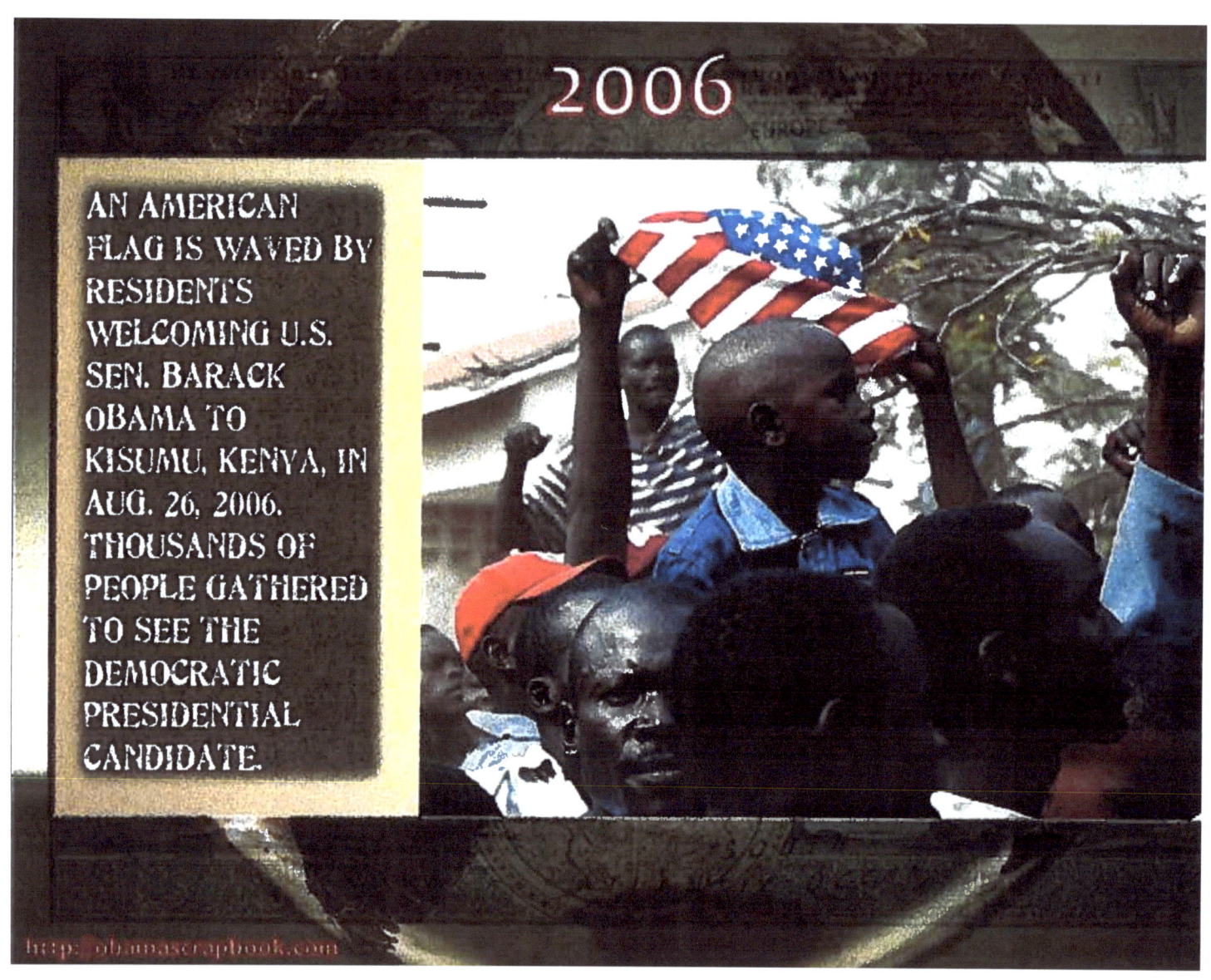

2006

AN AMERICAN FLAG IS WAVED BY RESIDENTS WELCOMING U.S. SEN. BARACK OBAMA TO KISUMU, KENYA, IN AUG. 26, 2006. THOUSANDS OF PEOPLE GATHERED TO SEE THE DEMOCRATIC PRESIDENTIAL CANDIDATE.

Obama speaks at a book-signing session on October 25, 2006 in San Rafael, California. Approximately 1,200 people packed the center's auditorium to have Obama sign copies of *The Audacity of Hope: Thoughts on Reclaiming the American Dream.*

YES, HE IS A STAR

OBAMA

Obama wears a cowboy hat offered by a supporter after speaking at an outdoor rally on February 23, 2007 in Austin

2007

http://obamascrapbook.com

48

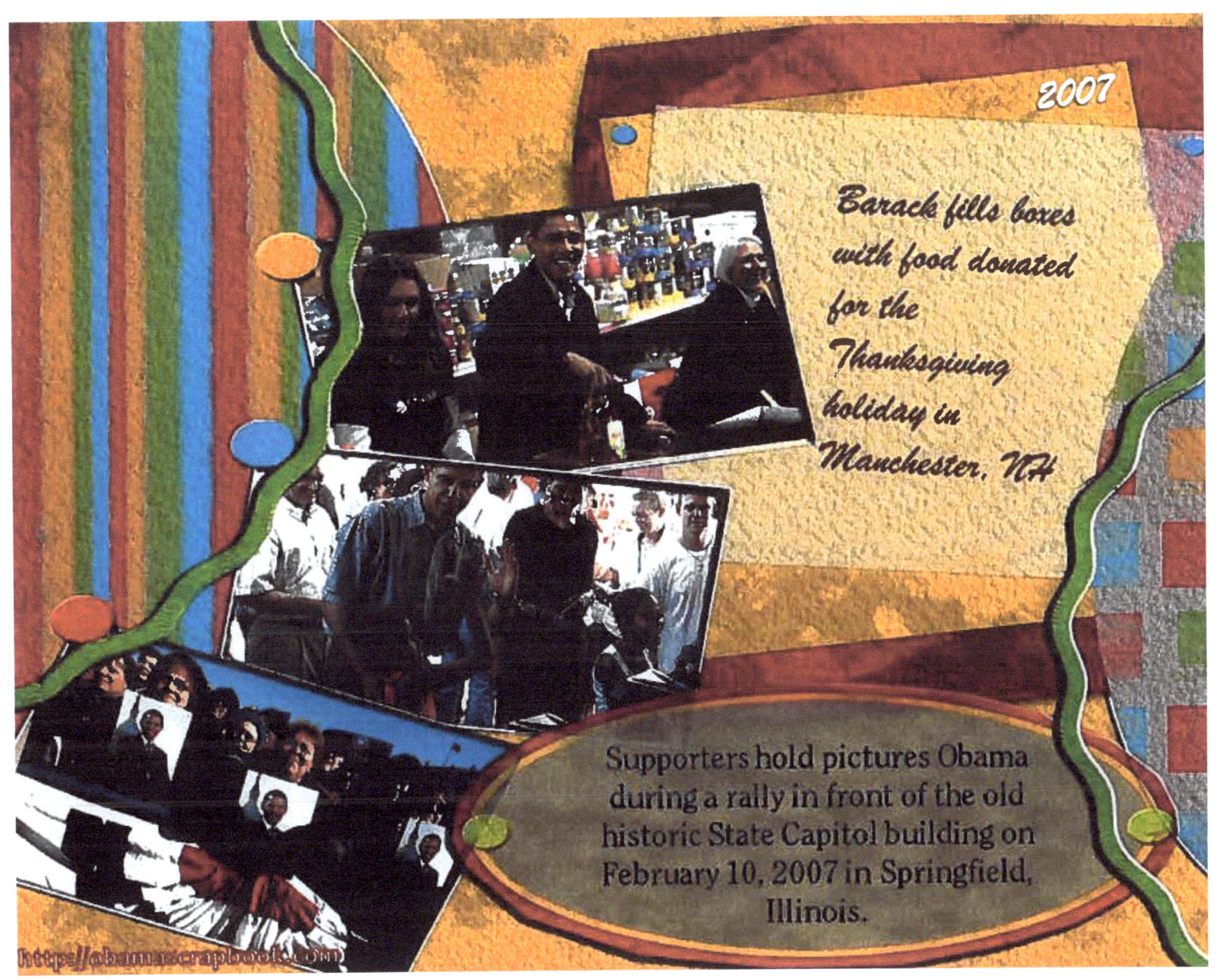

2007

Barack fills boxes with food donated for the Thanksgiving holiday in Manchester, NH

Supporters hold pictures Obama during a rally in front of the old historic State Capitol building on February 10, 2007 in Springfield, Illinois.

http://obamascrapbook.com

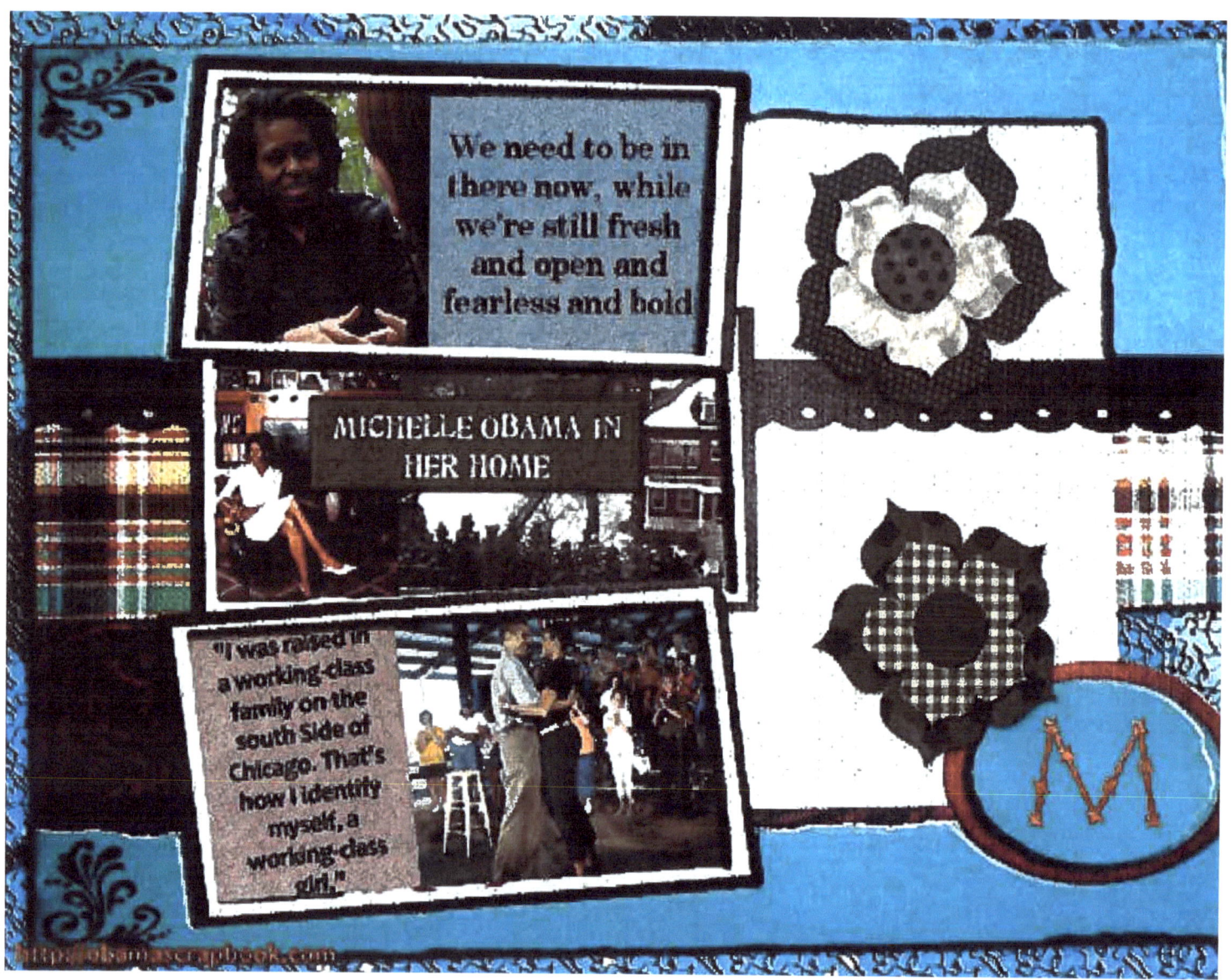

We need to be in there now, while we're still fresh and open and fearless and bold

MICHELLE OBAMA IN HER HOME

"I was raised in a working-class family on the south Side of Chicago. That's how I identify myself, a working-class girl."

http://obamascrapbook.com

50

Obama shakes hands after delivering a speech at the Miami Dade County Auditorium on August 25, 2007 in Miami

Obama waves to the crowd while Oprah Winfrey and his wife Michelle look on at a campaign event on December 9, 2007 in Manchester, New Hampshire

2007

Senator Obama poses with a tiny puppy mill survivor, Baby, in front of the Lincoln Memorial.

SENATOR BARACK OBAMA LAID
A WREATH AT THE TOMB OF
THE REV. DR. MARTIN LUTHER
KING JR. AND CORETTA SCOTT
KING AFTER SPEAKING AT
EBENEZER BAPTIST CHURCH IN
ATLANTA.

http://obamascrapbook.com

56

57

70

What must it feel like?

To carry the hopes and dreams of an entire race of people on your shoulders?

As much as I hate to say it, I know beyond a doubt that the next four weeks are going to be nasty. He's leading, and there are people who simply cannot stomach the idea of his beautiful family living in the White House. There will be smears, all sorts of slander and lies, the likes of which you've probably rarely seen. So y'all, we got to pray for this man. And please . . . make sure you VOTE!!! Vote early if you can!

November 5, 2008 , 12:06 am

Barack Obama's Victory Speech

Below are **Barack Obama**'s remarks as prepared for delivery tonight in Chicago:

If there is anyone out there who still doubts that America is a place where all things are possible; who still wonders if the dream of our founders is alive in our time; who still questions the power of our democracy, tonight is your answer.

It's the answer told by lines that stretched around schools and churches in numbers this nation has never seen; by people who waited three hours and four hours, many for the very first time in their lives, because they believed that this time must be different; that their voice could be that difference.

It's the answer spoken by young and old, rich and poor, Democrat and Republican, black, white, Latino, Asian, Native American, gay, straight, disabled and not disabled — Americans who sent a message to the world that we have never been a collection of red states and blue states; we are, and always will be, the United States of America.

It's the answer that led those who have been told for so long by so many to be cynical, and fearful, and doubtful of what we can achieve to put their hands on the arc of history and bend it once more toward the hope of a better day.

It's been a long time coming, but tonight, because of what we did on this day, in this election, at this defining moment, change has come to America.

I just received a very gracious call from Sen. McCain. He fought long and hard in this campaign, and he's fought even longer and harder for the country he loves. He has endured sacrifices for America that most of us cannot begin to imagine, and we are better off for the service rendered by this brave and selfless leader. I congratulate him and Gov. Palin for all they have achieved, and I look forward to working with them to renew this nation's promise in the months ahead.

I want to thank my partner in this journey, a man who campaigned from his heart and spoke for the men and women he grew up with on the streets of Scranton and rode with on that train home to Delaware, the vice-president-elect of the United States, Joe Biden.

I would not be standing here tonight without the unyielding support of my best friend for the last 16 years, the rock of our family and the love of my life, our nation's next first lady, Michelle Obama. Sasha and Malia, I love you both so much, and you have earned the new puppy that's coming with us to the White House. And while she's no longer with us, I know my grandmother is watching, along with the family that made me who I am. I miss them tonight, and know that my debt to them is beyond measure.

To my campaign manager, David Plouffe; my chief strategist, David Axelrod; and the best campaign team ever assembled in the history of politics — you made this happen, and I am forever grateful for what you've sacrificed to get it done.

But above all, I will never forget who this victory truly belongs to — it belongs to you.

I was never the likeliest candidate for this office. We didn't start with much money or many endorsements. Our campaign was not hatched in the halls of Washington — it began in the backyards of Des Moines and the living rooms of Concord and the front porches of Charleston.

It was built by working men and women who dug into what little savings they had to give $5 and $10 and $20 to this cause. It grew strength from the young people who rejected the myth of their generation's apathy; who left their homes and their families for jobs that offered little pay and less sleep; from the not-so-young people who braved the bitter cold and scorching heat to knock on the doors of perfect strangers; from the millions of Americans who volunteered and organized, and proved that more than two centuries later, a government of the people, by the people and for the people has not perished from this earth. This is your victory.

I know you didn't do this just to win an election, and I know you didn't do it for me. You did it because you understand the enormity of the task that lies ahead. For even as we celebrate tonight, we know the challenges that tomorrow will bring are the greatest of our lifetime — two wars, a planet in peril, the worst financial crisis in a century. Even as we stand here tonight, we know there are brave Americans waking up in the deserts of Iraq and the mountains of Afghanistan to risk their lives for us. There are mothers and fathers who will lie awake after their children fall asleep and wonder how they'll make the mortgage, or pay their doctor's bills, or save enough for college. There is new energy to harness and new jobs to be created; new schools to build and threats to meet and alliances to repair.

The road ahead will be long. Our climb will be steep. We may not get there in one year, or even one term, but America — I have never been more hopeful than I am tonight that we will get there. I promise you: We as a people will get there.

There will be setbacks and false starts. There are many who won't agree with every decision or policy I make as president, and we know that government can't solve every problem. But I will always be honest with you about the challenges we face. I will listen to you, especially when we disagree. And, above all, I will ask you join in the work of remaking this nation the only way it's been done in America for

221 years — block by block, brick by brick, callused hand by callused hand.

What began 21 months ago in the depths of winter must not end on this autumn night. This victory alone is not the change we seek — it is only the chance for us to make that change. And that cannot happen if we go back to the way things were. It cannot happen without you.

So let us summon a new spirit of patriotism; of service and responsibility where each of us resolves to pitch in and work harder and look after not only ourselves, but each other. Let us remember that if this financial crisis taught us anything, it's that we cannot have a thriving Wall Street while Main Street suffers. In this country, we rise or fall as one nation — as one people.

Let us resist the temptation to fall back on the same partisanship and pettiness and immaturity that has poisoned our politics for so long. Let us remember that it was a man from this state who first carried the banner of the Republican Party to the White House — a party founded on the values of self-reliance, individual liberty and national unity. Those are values we all share, and while the Democratic Party has won a great victory tonight, we do so with a measure of humility and determination to heal the divides that have held back our progress.

As Lincoln said to a nation far more divided than ours, "We are not enemies, but friends... Though passion may have strained, it must not break our bonds of affection." And, to those Americans whose support I have yet to earn, I may not have won your vote, but I hear your voices, I need your help, and I will be your president, too.

And to all those watching tonight from beyond our shores, from parliaments and palaces to those who are huddled around radios in the forgotten corners of our world — our stories are singular, but our destiny is shared, and a new dawn of American leadership is at hand. To those who would tear this world down: We will defeat you. To those who seek peace and security: We support you. And to all those who have wondered if America's beacon still burns as bright: Tonight, we proved once more that the true strength of our nation comes not from the might of our arms or the scale of our wealth, but from the enduring power of our ideals: democracy, liberty, opportunity and unyielding hope.

For that is the true genius of America — that America can change. Our union can be perfected. And what we have already achieved gives us hope for what we can and must achieve tomorrow.

This election had many firsts and many stories that will be told for generations. But one that's on my mind tonight is about a woman who cast her ballot in Atlanta. She's a lot like the millions of others who stood in line to make their voice heard in this election, except for one thing: Ann Nixon Cooper is 106 years old.

She was born just a generation past slavery; a time when there were no cars on the road or planes in the sky; when someone like her couldn't vote for two reasons — because she was a woman and because of the color of her skin.

And tonight, I think about all that she's seen throughout her century in America — the heartache and the hope; the struggle and the progress; the times we were told that we can't and the people who pressed on with that American creed: Yes, we can.

At a time when women's voices were silenced and their hopes dismissed, she lived to see them stand up and speak out and reach for the ballot. Yes, we can.

When there was despair in the Dust Bowl and depression across the land, she saw a nation conquer fear itself with a New Deal, new jobs and a new sense of common purpose. Yes, we can.

When the bombs fell on our harbor and tyranny threatened the world, she was there to witness a generation rise to greatness and a democracy was saved. Yes, we can.

She was there for the buses in Montgomery, the hoses in Birmingham, a bridge in Selma and a preacher from Atlanta who told a people that "We Shall Overcome." Yes, we can.

A man touched down on the moon, a wall came down in Berlin, a world was connected by our own science and imagination. And this year, in this election, she touched her finger to a screen and cast her vote, because after 106 years in America, through the best of times and the darkest of hours, she knows how America can change. Yes, we can.

America, we have come so far. We have seen so much. But there is so much more to do. So tonight, let us ask ourselves: If our children should live to see the next century; if my daughters should be so lucky to live as long as Ann Nixon Cooper, what change will they see? What progress will we have made?

This is our chance to answer that call. This is our moment. This is our time — to put our people back to work and open doors of opportunity for our kids; to restore prosperity and promote the cause of peace; to reclaim the American Dream and reaffirm that fundamental truth that out of many, we are one; that while we breathe, we hope, and where we are met with cynicism, and doubt, and those who tell us that we can't, we will respond with that timeless creed that sums up the spirit of a people: Yes, we can.

Thank you, God bless you, and may God bless the United States of America.

ELECTION SPECIAL | Commemorative Edition

Weather
Today: Rain. High 64.
Low 51.
Thursday: Mostly cloudy.
Low 63. High 52.

The Washington Post

NEWSSTAND $1.50

WEDNESDAY, NOVEMBER 5, 2008

Obama Makes History

U.S. DECISIVELY ELECTS FIRST BLACK PRESIDENT

DEMOCRATS EXPAND CONTROL OF CONGRESS

By Robert Barnes and Michael D. Shear
Washington Post Staff Writers

President-elect Barack Obama, with wife Michelle and their daughters, Sasha, 7, and Malia, 10, greets a crowd of 125,000 celebrating his victory in Grant Park, in his home town of Chicago.

Sen. Barack Obama of Illinois was elected the nation's 44th president yesterday, riding a reformist message of change and an inspirational exhortation of hope to become the first African American to ascend to the White House.

Obama, 47, the son of a Kenyan father and a white mother from Kansas, led a tide of Democratic victories across the nation in defeating Republican Sen. John McCain of Arizona, a 26-year veteran of Washington who could not overcome his connections to President Bush's increasingly unpopular administration.

Standing before a crowd of more than 125,000 people who had waited for hours at Chicago's Grant Park, Obama acknowledged the accomplishment and the dreams of his supporters.

"If there is anyone out there who still doubts that America is a place where all things are possible, who still wonders if the dream of our founders is alive in our time, who still questions the power of our democracy, tonight is your answer," he said just before midnight Eastern time.

"The road ahead will be long. Our climb will be steep. We may not get there in one year or even one term, but America, I have never been more hopeful than I am tonight that we will get there. I promise you: We as a people will get there."

The historic Election Day brought millions of new and sometimes tearful voters, long lines at polling places nationwide, and celebrations on street corners and in front of the White House. It ushered in a new era of Democratic dominance in Congress, even though the party's quest for the 60 votes needed for a veto-proof majority in the Senate remained in doubt early today. In the House, Democrats made major gains, adding to their already sizable advantage and returning them to a position of power that predates the 1994 Re-

See ELECTION, A16, Col. 1

HOW HE WON

Measured Response To Financial Crisis Sealed the Election

By Anne E. Kornblut
Washington Post Staff Writer

Sen. Barack Obama, so steady in public, did not hide his vexation when he summoned his top advisers to meet with him in Chicago on Sept. 14.

His general-election campaign had gone stale. For weeks, he had watched Sen. John McCain suction up the oxygen in the race, driving the news coverage after the boisterous Republican convention in St. Paul, Minn., and suddenly drawing huge crowds with his new running mate, Alaska Gov. Sarah Palin.

Convening the meeting that Sunday in the office of David Axelrod, his chief strategist, Obama was blunt: It was time to get serious.

"He said, 'You know, maybe we can just win it on the issues. But I don't think so,' " recalled senior adviser Anita Dunn. With the debates approaching and just seven weeks until the election, "his charge to everybody was 'Guys, we're back in combat mode,' " Dunn said.

And then, the next morning, a global earthquake hit: Lehman Brothers, the giant investment firm, filed for bankruptcy, triggering the biggest corporate collapse in U.S. history and an international financial meltdown, and transforming the presidential race.

It was a moment neither the senator from Illinois nor his advisers had anticipated, but one for which they were uniquely prepared. In the days that followed, the newly chastised Obama team became more aggressive, with a message they had refined over the summer. The candidate himself, criticized as too cool, too cerebral and too detached, suddenly had the opportunity to show

See OBAMA, A12, Col. 1

At Busboys and Poets in the District, Tiffany Payton and Barbara Mack, right, embrace as Obama is declared the winner.

A DAY OF TRANSFORMATION

America's History Gives Way to Its Future

By Kevin Merida
Washington Post Staff Writer

After a day of runaway lines that circled blocks, of ladies hobbling on canes and drummers rollicking on street corners, the enormous significance of Barack Obama's election finally began to sink into the landscape. The magnitude of his win suggested that the country itself might be in a gravitational pull toward a rebirth that some were slow to recognize.

Tears flowed, not only for Obama's historic achievement, but because many were happily discovering that perhaps they had underestimated possibility in America.

When the novelist Kim McLarin watched her vote being recorded at her polling station in Milton, Mass., she stood still for a moment with her 8-year-old son, Isaac. "My heart was full. I could scarcely breathe," she said. "What I've been

forced to acknowledge is there has been a shift — it's not a sea change. But there's been a decided shift in the meaning of race. It's not an ending. It's a beginning."

What kind of beginning it is, Americans were wrestling with late into the night, some popping champagne and others burdened with unease. Would enduring strains of intolerance lose their power or gain rebellious steam? Could new hope be harnessed to create new solutions? Is America ready to pull itself together or resigned to live divided? The campaign that began for Obama 21 months ago had raised in stark terms whether America was ready for a black president. Last night's answer — a resounding yes — raises the next question: How much more change will America embrace?

When McLarin learned last night that the nation had voted

See TRANSFORMATION, A11, Col. 1

THE AGENDA

Hard Choices And Challenges Follow Triumph

By Dan Balz
Washington Post Staff Writer

After a victory of historic significance, Barack Obama will inherit problems of historic proportions. Not since Franklin D. Roosevelt was inaugurated at the depths of the Great Depression in 1933 has a new president been confronted with the challenges Obama will face as he starts his presidency.

At home, Obama must revive an economy experiencing some of the worst shocks in more than half a century. Abroad, he has pledged to end the war in Iraq and defeat al-Qaeda and the Taliban in Afghanistan. He can run a platform to change the country and its politics. Now he must begin to spell out exactly how.

Obama's winning percentage appears likely to be the largest of any Democrat since Lyndon Johnson's 1964 landslide and makes him the first since Jimmy Carter in 1976 to garner more than 50.1 percent. Like Johnson, he will govern with sizable congressional majorities. Democrats gained at least five seats in the Senate and looked to add significantly to their strength in the House.

But with those advantages come hard choices. Among them will be deciding how much he owes his victory to a popular rejection of President Bush and the Republicans and how much it represents an embrace of Democratic governance. Interpreting his mandate will be only one of several critical decisions Obama must make as he prepares

See AGENDA, A8, Col. 1

WEDNESDAY, NOVEMBER 5, 2008

Los Angeles Times

latimes.com

IT'S OBAMA

DECISIVE VICTORY MAKES HISTORY

In California, gay-marriage ban takes early lead

'CHANGE HAS COME': President-elect Barack Obama celebrates with his wife, Michelle, their daughters, Sasha and Malia, and more than 200,000 supporters gathered along Chicago's waterfront. Many wept at the landmark moment.

The first black president-elect wins a solid mandate and a fortified Democratic majority in Congress.

MARK Z. BARABAK

Barack Obama, the son of a father from Kenya and a white mother from Kansas, was elected the nation's 44th president Tuesday, breaking the ultimate racial barrier to become the first African American to claim the country's highest office.

A nation founded by slave owners and seared by civil war and generations of racial strife delivered a smashing electoral college victory to the 47-year-old first-term senator from Illinois, who forged a broad, multiracial, multiethnic coalition. His victory was a leap in the march toward equality: When Obama was born, people with his skin color could not even vote in parts of America, and many were killed for trying.

"If there is anyone out there who still doubts that America is a place where all things are possible, who still wonders if the dream of our founders is alive in our time, who still questions the power of our democracy, tonight is your answer," Obama told more than 200,000 celebrants gathered along Chicago's waterfront. Many had tears streaking their faces.

"It's been a long time coming," said Obama, who strode on stage with his wife, Michelle, and their two daughters, Sasha and Malia. "But tonight, because of what we did on this day, in this election, at this defining moment, change has come to America."

Obama was beating Republican John McCain in every state Democrats carried four years ago, including Pennsylvania, which McCain had worked vigorously to pry away. Obama also made significant inroads into Republican turf, carrying Ohio, Colorado and Virginia, the latter voted Democratic for the first time in more than 40 years. He won the swing states of Florida, New Hampshire, Iowa and New Mexico, which backed President Bush in 2004.

In winning the White House, Obama to a large degree remade the electorate. About 1 in 10 of those casting ballots Tuesday were doing so for the first time. Though that number [See Election, Page A8]

"Whatever our differences, we are fellow Americans," John McCain conceded.

NEWS ANALYSIS

Now it's idealism versus realism

DOYLE McMANUS
REPORTING FROM WASHINGTON

Barack Obama won the presidency Tuesday by persuading voters to embrace a seeming paradox: leadership based on contradictory principles of change and reassurance.

The Illinois senator combined ambitious goals and a cautious temperament. He promised tax cuts, better healthcare, new energy programs and fiscal discipline all at the same time, and all with out the bitterness and stalemate that arose when these issues were tackled in the past.

Now, as Obama moves through his transition to the White House, this effort to square the political circle becomes the defining challenge in the months ahead. Which Barack Obama will dominate as he begins to govern?

Too much of the ambitious [See Analysis, Page A11]

Nation watches as state weighs ban

Prop. 8 battle drew money and attention from across the U.S.

JESSICA GARRISON, CARA MIA DiMASSA AND RICHARD PADDOCK

A measure to ban gay marriage in California led in early returns Tuesday although the final outcome remained in doubt, leaving advocates on both sides in suspense about the most divisive and emotionally fraught contest in the state this year.

Proposition 8 would amend the California Constitution to define marriage as being only between a man and a woman.

Proposition 8 was the most expensive proposition on any ballot in the nation this year, with more than $74 million spent by both sides.

The measure's most fervent proponents believed that nothing less than the future of traditional families was at stake, while opponents believed that they were fighting for the fundamental right of gay people to be treated equally under the law.

In San Francisco, supporters of gay marriage packed a ballroom at the Westin St. Francis Hotel on Tuesday night.

"You divided to lose your life out loud. You fell in love and you said 'I do.' Tonight, we await a verdict," San Francisco Mayor Gavin Newsom told a crowd.

[See Prop. 8, Page A21]

PROPOSITION 8
Eliminate gay marriage

YES	NO
52.5%	47.5%

Results as of 11:57 p.m. Pacific Time with 37% of precincts reporting.

ELECTORAL VOTES
270 needed to win

OBAMA	McCAIN	UNDECIDED
349	144	45

111TH CONGRESS
The House of Representatives
218 seats to control the House

DEMOCRATS	REPUBLICANS	UNDECIDED
242	160	33

The Senate
51 seats to control the Senate

DEMOCRATS	REPUBLICANS	UNDECIDED
56*	40	4

* Includes 2 independents. All results as of 11:10 p.m. Pacific time

Analysis: Erasing race assumptions
Even in Virginia, heart of the Confederacy, Obama prevails. A11

They wouldn't miss this for the world
Voters turn out in droves to take their part in history. A16

Roundup of state propositions
Measures on redistricting and farm animals are ahead. A20

latimes.com

All the latest news
View interactive maps detailing results for elections around the country and for all statewide measures and propositions.

Where hope has wrestled with fear

SANDY BANKS
REPORTING FROM CLEVELAND

I could not have imagined that less than four years later, he would be elected president.

His name was so seductive, I kept stumbling over it during our 45-minute interview about the role of race in his life and in his politics. Was it Barack Obama or oBama Barack?

The next morning, unbidden, he called me back.

"Hey Sandy," he said. "This is Barack. I've been thinking about what we talked about, and I wanted to add some thoughts."

By the time we finished our second chat, there were two things I thought I knew.

Barack Obama was determined to force this country to confront its "legacy of slavery."

And what he was asking — and offering — was too much for a nation still bitterly divided by skin color.

"His candidacy would make this country squirm and shudder and maybe even come unglued," I wrote back then.

Clearly, I underestimated him — and us.

How could I have been so wrong? Last week, as Obama closed in on the presidency, I went back to my hometown to look for answers.

Cleveland was a steppingstone for my parents. My father's family fled Georgia in the 1930s, one step ahead of a lynch mob set on teaching my uncle a lesson for daring to sass a white man. Twenty years later, my mother led her siblings north from a farm in Alabama, after my father in Cleveland. They married, and I was the eldest.

[See Banks, Page A12]

Weather Page B10
Complete Index A2

TODAY'S INSIDE SECTIONS
California, Business,
Sports, Calendar and Food

Printed with soy inks on partially recycled paper

7 85944 00050 6

100

VOLUME 274
NUMBER 119

75 cents

The Boston Globe

WEDNESDAY, NOVEMBER 5, 2008

Historic victory

ELECTORAL COLLEGE · Obama 338 · 142 · 270 NEEDED TO WIN

Obama elected nation's first African-American president in a romp

McCain falters on GOP terrain; Democrats increase clout in Congress

President-elect Barack Obama, his daughters Sasha and Malia, and wife Michelle waved to supporters last night in Chicago's Grant Park.

By Scott Helman and Michael Kranish

CHICAGO — Senator Barack Obama of Illinois was elected the 44th president of the United States and the nation's first black commander in chief yesterday, his triumph ushering in an era of profound political and social realignment in America.

Obama's decisive victory over Republican John McCain is a landmark in the country's 232-year history, especially for the millions of African-Americans around the country energized and inspired by his improbable candidacy. It gives Democrats control of Congress and the White House for the first time in 16 years and led to spontaneous celebrations around the country.

Making good on his promise to draw his own electoral map, Obama captured Virginia which last voted for a Democrat in 1964, and he beat McCain in key battleground states, including Colorado, Florida, New Hampshire, Ohio, and Pennsylvania, while holding on to Democratic-leaning states. He won in part on the support of new voters, African-Americans, and Hispanics, and as of early today he had 338 electoral votes, far more than the 270 needed to win the presidency while McCain had 142.

In a grand celebration on a balmy fall night in Chicago's Grant Park, 240,000 supporters gathered to toast the president-elect. When the networks called the race shortly after 10 p.m. local time, tears flowed, flashbulbs...

ELECTION, Page A12

New era beginning for party in power

By Susan Milligan

WASHINGTON — Democrats increased their ranks in Congress last night, picking up seats from the Canadian to the Mexican borders and ushering in a new era of Democratic power in Washington the party has not seen since the 1990s.

In a heavy blow to the GOP, Democrats collected several high-profile female seats, ousting veteran Republican lawmaker John Sununu in New Hampshire and replacing him with former governor Jeanne Shaheen. New Mexico and Colorado sent two Democratic brothers to the Senate, with Mark Udall taking the Colorado seat and Tom Udall winning the seat in New Mexico.

In Virginia, Mark Warner easily defeated James Gilmore, his GOP opponent, capping a stunning Democratic showing in the Old Dominion State, which also voted for Barack Obama — the first time since 1964 that a Democratic president...

CONGRESS, Page A13

boston.com

ELECTORAL COLLEGE · Obama · McCain · Not decided

Election 2008

John McCain said he gave his all, while aides said his trouble began when he declared the teetering economy sound. A14.

Lines were long at polling places across the nation, but Obama's prodigious field organization helped keep problems to a minimum. A16.

Massachusetts voters rejected a repeal of the state income tax, decriminalized possession of small amounts of marijuana, and approved a ban on greyhound racing. B1.

Senator John F. Kerry easily won reelection to a fifth term, fending off a challenge by Republican Jeffrey K. Beatty. B6.

NEWS ANALYSIS

Shift in tone will bring a watershed for nation

By Peter Canellos

CHICAGO — The people who crowded Grant Park last night, straining for a glimpse of President-elect Barack Obama, were aroused by a lot of passions — war, race, jobs, race — and yet they insisted that no single goal, nothing that could be written out and measured, defined their expectations for the next administration.

"It's everything," said a tearful Teri McClain of Seattle.

"It's having a president with a world view that most Americans can believe in," declared Chris Godfrey of Des Moines, Iowa.

And yet Obama's clear-cut victory, bolstered by strong majorities of his own party in both houses of Congress, can be read as a mandate for some very specific policy changes that could, by themselves, have momentous import. Withdrawal from Iraq. Renewal of the six-decade quest for national health insurance. The launch of a major government-funded quest for renewable energy.

Beyond the politics, Obama's election will stand forever amid the great milestones of America's racial history, the end of a tortuous progression from enslavement to the civil rights movement to the election of the first black...

ANALYSIS, Page A17

Among blacks, joy and tears at journey's end

By Michael Levenson

Sixty-six-year-old John Dooley picked cotton as a boy in Beaufort, S.C., just as his father and grandfather did before him. So yesterday, as he stood amid a throng of people hugging, high-fiving, and even weeping outside a Roxbury polling place, he wanted to underscore the significance of the day.

"This," he said to a little boy, grabbing her head and staring deeply into her eyes, "is history."

At another polling station blocks away, Charles Robinson recalled the racial epithets shouted at him as a student at South Boston High School during the...

BLACK VOTE, Page A17

Chicago Tribune

WEDNESDAY, NOVEMBER 5, 2008 ONLINE AT CHICAGOTRIBUNE.COM

THE CITY & SUBURBS, $1.00 ELSEWHERE · 146NE YEAR NO. 310 © CHICAGO TRIBUNE   C CN CS N NNW NRW NS NW S SSW W

Enormous turnout propels
Illinois senator to victory
as the first African-American
elected president

It's Obama

Supporters at the rally in Grant Park on Tuesday night react upon hearing that Barack Obama had won Pennsylvania. **PHIL VELASQUEZ/TRIBUNE**

Barack Obama, son of an African man and a white woman from Kansas, a figure virtually unknown outside his home state of Illinois just five years ago, emphatically captured the presidency Tuesday night, as crowds massed in Grant Park to cheer his victory.

His improbable journey to become the nation's first black president began on a cold February day almost two years ago, as he offered himself as a candidate. Obama had spent little time on the national stage and was the farthest thing from a traditional candidate. Among other things, he was an African American in a country still grappling with the question of race.

With his victory, America's tortured relationship with race has entered a new phase. The Obama presidency may be a sign that a country that all too recently tolerated segregation has moved irrevocably forward, or it may mean only that the nation is so hungry for change that it set aside racial struggles.

Obama is a man of extraordinary political gifts. The challenges facing him are many, including wars in Iraq and Afghanistan, and a struggling economy. He will confront them soon enough.

But Tuesday night, at least, was a time to marvel at a once-inconceivable moment in American history.

COMPLETE ELECTION COVERAGE INSIDE

Austin American-Statesman

statesman.com   STATE EDITION • WEDNESDAY, NOVEMBER 5, 2008 • 75 CENTS

IT'S OBAMA
U.S. ELECTS ITS FIRST BLACK PRESIDENT

'Change has come,' President-elect Barack Obama told supporters at a celebration in Chicago. He asked Americans to "summon a new spirit of patriotism, of service and responsibility."

Voters embrace Democrat's message of change

By Scott Shepard
WASHINGTON BUREAU

CHICAGO — An unhappy and unsettled America picked an unlikely president Tuesday: Sen. Barack Obama, a 47-year-old African American lawmaker from Illinois who sparked a sweeping political movement with an eloquent promise of change and, one rim perversely, hope.

"Yes, we can," Obama said repeatedly during a speech for the presidency that lasted almost two years, through brutal and democratic Party primaries. A costly war on two fronts in the Middle East, economic woes that have been compared to the Great Depression of the 1930s and questions about his patriotism.

In the end, despite lingering questions about his some experience, especially on the world stage, Obama defeated veteran Republican Sen. John McCain in an election heralding what could be a redefining moment in the history of America.

Television networks declared Obama the winner about 10 p.m. Central Standard Time as polls closed on the West Coast, where Obama was heavily favored after he piled up electoral votes to reach the 270-vote threshold to become the first black president in the country's history.

Analysts said Obama's success was added in part by the public's displeasure with President Bush, whose pre-election approval rating bottomed out at 18 percent, the lowest the Gallup Polling Organization ever recorded for a modern president.

Obama carried some of the states that were key to Bush's re-election four years ago, most notably Ohio, Florida, New Mexico and Iowa. And he and McCain were locked in a close battle for the Republican stronghold of Indiana.

"At this point we need a miracle," a McCain aide was quoted as saying on the CBS News Web site after Ohio fell. No Republican has won the presidency without carrying Ohio.

A victory for McCain would have been historic as well. The 72-year-old senator would have been the oldest president to begin a first term in the White House and the first Vietnam War veteran to serve in the Oval Office. His running mate, Alaska Gov. Sarah Palin, would have been the first female U.S. vice president.

Obama also won Pennsylvania, a Democratic leaning state McCain had targeted with time and money. Without Pennsylvania, it would

See **ELECTED**, A13

CONGRESSIONAL RACES
Democrats gain ground in both Senate and House

By Carl Hulse
THE NEW YORK TIMES

Democrats scored some quick and convincing victories Tuesday in both houses of Congress, picking up Senate seats in North Carolina, New Hampshire and Virginia in what party officials hoped were the first steps toward increasing the numbers on Capitol Hill to pursue an ambitious policy agenda.

All 435 House seats and 35 Senate seats were at stake, but incumbents were expected to be easy to re-election in most of those races, putting the focus on about a dozen Senate seats and 30 House seats where the competition was fierce.

In North Carolina, Sen. Elizabeth Dole, one of the most famous names in Republican politics, was defeated by Kay Hagan, a state lawmaker whose portrayal of Dole as a Washington insider suggested that she was out of touch with the people of her state.

See **WINS**, A16

Republican Sen. John McCain, with wife Cindy McCain, thanked supporters of his presidential campaign and congratulated Barack Obama for his victory at a Phoenix, Ariz., rally on Tuesday night.

ANALYSIS
Winning was hard, but tough tasks of leading lie ahead

By Liz Sidoti
ASSOCIATED PRESS

WASHINGTON — Now comes the hard part.

Democratic Sen. Barack Obama bore the Democrats' unstinting confidence and doubts about his experience and overcame questions about his race to be elected the first black president of the United States.

As president-elect, he faces three immediate challenges: confronting the worst economic conditions since the Great Depression, down-winding the next steps in two lingering wars and keeping his Democrats, including some who want the change he has promised to come instantly. It won't.

On the heels of a campaign in which cash wasn't a concern, Obama must tackle all those tasks in little months in the budget as the nation appears to be heading for a painful recession.

See **FUTURE**, A12

MARLAND WEEKLY   INSIDE ● BUSINESS B1-7 ● DEATHS B3-4 ● EDITORIALS A20-21 ● FOOD & LIFE D1 ● SPORTS C1 ● WORLD & NATION A2 ● CLASSIFIEDS E1
IN METRO & STATE ● FEMALE UT FACULTY MEMBERS TRAIL MALE COUNTERPARTS IN PAY AND STATUS, GENDER EQUITY TASK FORCE SAYS ● B1

TO SUBSCRIBE
Call 445-4040

104

The Times-Picayune

nola BREAKING NEWS AT NOLA.COM | WEDNESDAY, NOVEMBER 5, 2008 | METRO EDITION · 75¢

THE 44th PRESIDENT

BARACK OBAMA	JOHN McCAIN
52% POPULAR	47% POPULAR
349 ELECTORAL	159 ELECTORAL

IN HISTORIC RUN, OBAMA WINS WHITE HOUSE

PHOTO BY PABLO MARTINEZ MONSIVAIS / THE ASSOCIATED PRESS

By Michael D. Shear and Robert Barnes The Washington Post

WASHINGTON

Sen. Barack Obama of Illinois was elected the nation's 44th president Tuesday, riding a reformist message of change and an inspirational exhortation of hope to become the first African-American to ascend to the White House.

Obama, 47, the son of a Kenyan father and a white mother from Kansas, led a tide of Democratic victories across the nation in defeating Republican Sen. John McCain of Arizona, a 26-year veteran of Washington who could not overcome his connections to President Bush's increasingly unpopular administration.

Standing before a crowd of more than 125,000 that had waited for hours at Chicago's Grant Park, Obama acknowledged the accomplishment and the dreams of his supporters.

"If there is anyone out there who still doubts that America is a place where all things are possible, who still wonders if the dream of our founders is alive in our time, who still questions the power of our democracy, tonight is your answer," he said just before 11 p.m.

"The road ahead will be long. Our climb will be steep. We may not get there in one year or even one term, but America, I have never been more hopeful than I am tonight that we will get there. I promise you: We as a people will get there."

The historic Election Day brought millions of new and sometimes tearful voters, long lines at polling places nationwide, and celebrations for myriad corners and in front of the White House. It ushered in a new era of Democratic dominance in Congress, even

See PRESIDENT, A-9

President-elect Barack Obama acknowledges the cheers and tears of thousands as he takes the stage at his election night party in Grant Park, Chicago, on Tuesday.

U.S. SENATE

MARY LANDRIEU	963,905	52%
JOHN KENNEDY	855,723	46%

Landrieu takes a third term

By Ed Anderson and Bill Barrow Capital bureau

Once targeted by national Republicans as the U.S. Senate's most vulnerable Democratic incumbent, Sen. Mary Landrieu defeated GOP state Treasurer John Kennedy on Tuesday to claim a third term.

Landrieu, who won by narrow margins in 1996 and 2002, took a slightly more comfortable victory against the backdrop of her diminished Democratic base of pre-Katrina New Orleans.

Joined by her large family and former

See LANDRIEU, A-15

HOUSE: 1ST DISTRICT

STEVE SCALISE	178,355	66%
JIM HARLAN	91,569	34%

Scalise wins 1st District

By Mary Sparacello Kenner bureau

U.S. Rep. Steve Scalise turned back an aggressive $1.3 million challenge from Jim Harlan on Tuesday to win a full term representing the congressional 1st District.

"This has been a hard-fought campaign," Scalise, 43, told backers at Andrea's restaurant in Metairie. "The last few months have been a really challenging time for my family."

Scalise, a Republican from Old Jefferson, served 12 years as a state legislator, then

See SCALISE, A-16

HOUSE: 2ND DISTRICT

WILLIAM JEFFERSON	83,211	55%
HELENA MORENO	65,530	44%

Jefferson beats Moreno

By Frank Donze and Michelle Krupa Staff writers

With his trial on federal corruption charges looming and questions swirling about his effectiveness in Congress, U.S. Rep. William Jefferson cruised to an easy victory Tuesday in the Democratic Party runoff for the 2nd Congressional District.

The decisive win over Helena Moreno, a former TV news anchor and political newcomer, ensures Jefferson a spot in the Dec. 6 general election. With two-thirds of the district's voters registered as Democrats,

See JEFFERSON, A-20

OTHER RACES

COMPLETE ELECTION COVERAGE BEGINS ON A-9

STATE PAGE A-25
ERIC SKRMETTA
PUBLIC SERVICE COMMISSION

JEFFERSON PARISH PAGE A-26
ELLEN KOVACH
24TH JUDICIAL DISTRICT COURT, DIVISION N

NEW ORLEANS PAGE A-22
LEON CANNIZZARO
DISTRICT ATTORNEY

ST. TAMMANY PARISH PAGE A-30
REJECTED
ONE-QUARTER-CENT SALES TAX

172ND YEAR
NO. 289

THE WALL STREET JOURNAL.

WEDNESDAY, NOVEMBER 5, 2008 · VOL. CCLII NO. 108

Obama Sweeps to Historic Victory

Nation Elects Its First African-American President Amid Record Turnout; Turmoil in Economy Dominates Voters' Concerns

BY JONATHAN WEISMAN
AND LAURA MECKLER

WASHINGTON—Sen. Barack Obama was elected the nation's first African-American president, defeating Sen. John McCain decisively Tuesday as voters surged to the polls in a presidential race that climaxed amid the worst financial crisis since the Great Depression.

WINNING SMILE: Sen. Barack Obama became the nation's first African-American president, riding a historic turnout amid voter discontent with the economy to defeat Sen. John McCain.

Obama
338
electoral votes

51% of popular vote

McCain
140
electoral votes

48% of popular vote

Democrats Expand Majorities In Congress

BY GREG HITT
AND BRODY MULLINS

WASHINGTON—Democrats strengthened their majorities in both houses of Congress and moved close to a level of domination in the Senate that could enable them to push through major legislation.

The New Landscape

- Gerald Seib on challenges for Democrats A6
- A battle for the soul of the Republican Party ...A5
- A momentous day for African-Americans A8
- See WSJ.com for full state-by-state election results.

What's News—

Business & Finance

World-Wide

As Economic Crisis Peaked, Tide Turned Against McCain

BY MONICA LANGLEY

Campaign Addicts Now Confront The Morning After

As Election Coverage Fades, News Junkies Break Old Habits; Getting to Know the Kids

BY KEVIN HELLIKER
AND DAVID KESMODEL

WORLD WISE:

When there is no wind, there is no wind energy. Morgan Stanley scrutinizes the landscape on the seemingly simple, but quite complex search for energy investments. To find the sound investments today, you need to be world wise.

Morgan Stanley

110

CALGARY HERALD

BREAKING NEWS AT CALGARYHERALD.COM

PROUDLY CALGARY SINCE 1883 ◆ Wednesday, January 21, 2009

SOUVENIR EDITION: 15 PAGES OF COVERAGE

'Hope over fear'

Obama ushers in a new era as 44th president of United States

INSIDE

111

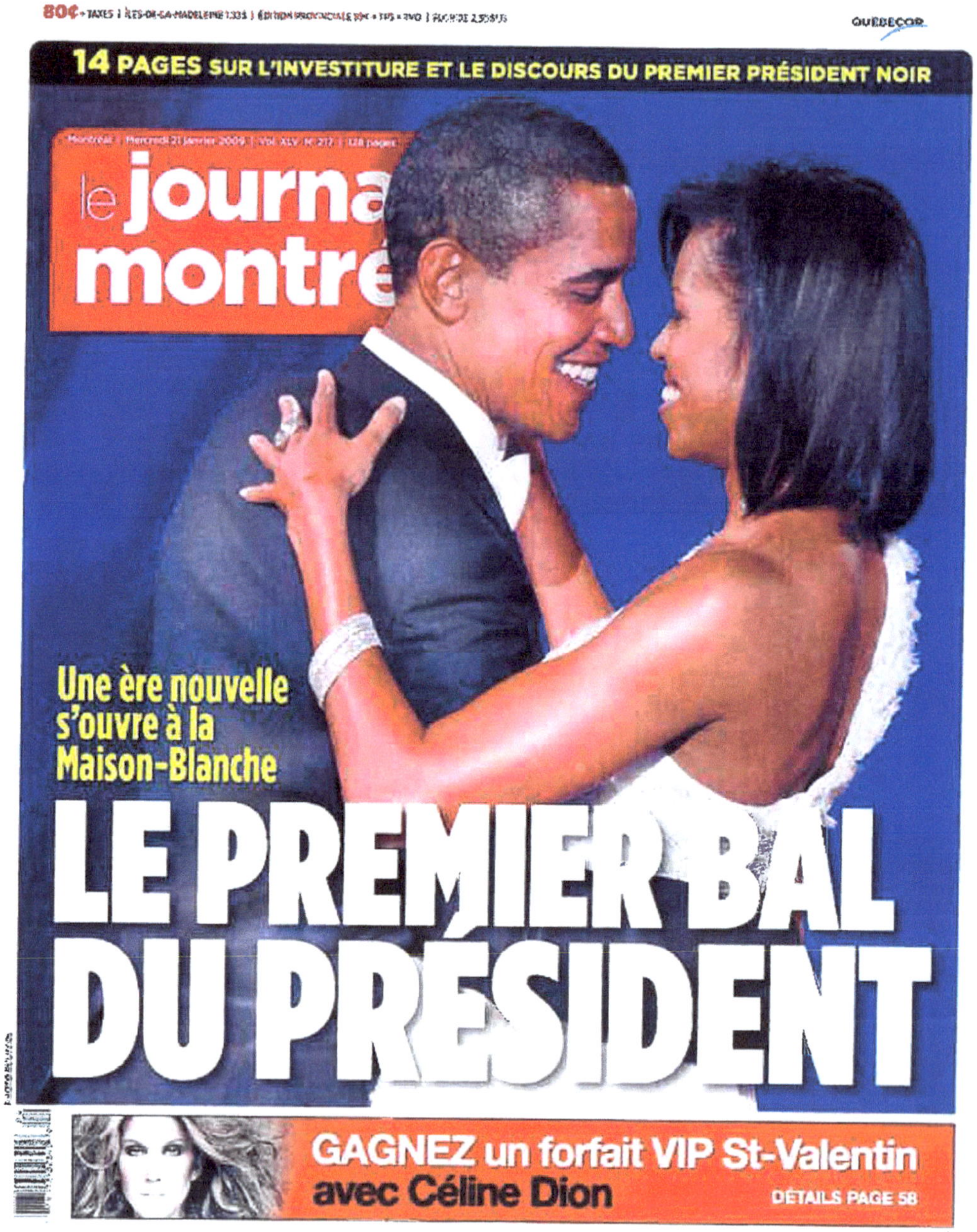
80¢ + TAXES | ÎLES-DE-LA-MADELEINE

QUEBECOR

14 PAGES SUR L'INVESTITURE ET LE DISCOURS DU PREMIER PRÉSIDENT NOIR

Montréal | Mercredi 21 janvier 2009 | Vol. XLV | N° 217 | 128 pages

le journa
montré

Une ère nouvelle s'ouvre à la Maison-Blanche

LE PREMIER BAL DU PRÉSIDENT

GAGNEZ un forfait VIP St-Valentin avec Céline Dion

DÉTAILS PAGE 58

High: -8
Low: -15
A frigid morning.
Chance of flurries
through evening.
Details: **Go 2**

THE HAMILTON
SPECTATOR

WEDNESDAY, JANUARY 21, 2009 ✦ THESPEC.COM ✦ THE VOICE OF OUR COMMUNITIES SINCE 1846

THE
PROMISE

'America is a friend of each nation and every man, woman and child
who seeks a future of peace and dignity'

114

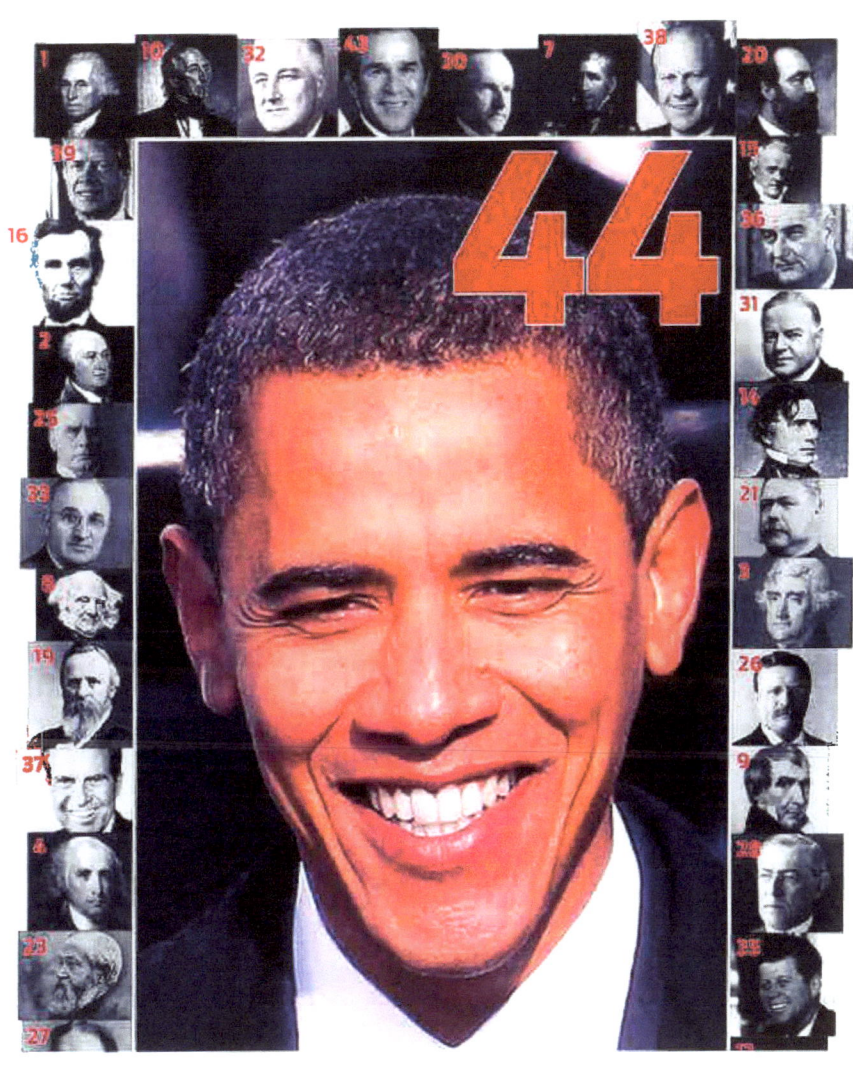

WEDNESDAY, JANUARY 21, 2009

THE DENVER POST

SO CENTS

"HOPE OVER FEAR"

THE INAUGURATION OF BARACK OBAMA

> This is the meaning of our liberty and our creed — why men and women and children of every race and every faith can join in celebration across this magnificent mall, and why a man whose father less than 60 years ago might not have been served at a local restaurant can now stand before you to take a most sacred oath."

With his wife, Michelle, holding the Bible and their daughters, Malia and Sasha, looking on, Barack Obama, the 47-year-old son of a white woman from Kansas and a black man from Africa, was sworn in by Chief Justice John Roberts a few minutes after noon EST. Chip Somodevilla, Getty Images

ANALYSIS

With reassurance and a call to action.

By Michael Riley The Denver Post

WASHINGTON» In the end, all the heraldry and Hollywood

The Journal

Wednesday January 21 2009 | www.journallive.co.uk | 50p

The moment that history was made

TAKING THE OATH Barack Obama watched by wife, Michelle, and daughters Malia and Sasha with Chief Justice John Roberts. Pages 8&9

'Brutal, global and exceptional'

Nissan boss warns that conditions are worst since 1929

THE chief executive of Nissan yesterday described the crisis facing European car manufacturers as the most severe since the Great Depression as he urged governments to step up their support for the sector.

Carlos Ghosn described the downturn as "brutal, global and of an exceptional size" as he laid bare the scale of the problems facing manufacturers at an industry summit in France. He call for greater state support for firms such as Nissan, which recently announced 1,200 job cuts in Sunderland, won backing from North politicians. Blaydon MP Dave Anderson said: "These comments reflect what a lot of us are feeling."

Full story 6&7

Hundreds of jobs on line at Alca...

HUNDREDS of jobs could be left hanging in the balance. The European Commission has filed papers with the European Court of Justice claiming the coal-fired plant in Lynemouth, Northumberland, has failed to meet emissions targets.
Page 25

CHARITY

Work of art will help Sir Bobby

CONTROVERSIAL artist Damien Hirst has donated a stunning circular work of art – worth more than £10,000 – to the Bobby Robson cancer charity. **Page 2**

Cause of tragedy is still a mystery

MYSTERY still surrounds a crash on the A696 last week which killed a nanny and seriously injured the little girl in her care. Yesterday an inquest into Moira Watson's death was told there was no obvious explanation why the car was on the wrong side of the road. **Page 4**

TODAY'S FORECAST

Mostly cloudy, cooler

High 72 — Low 53

Wednesday
January 21, 2009

50 Cents

Daily News

DailyNews.com

16-PAGE INAUGURATION SECTION BEGINS ON A21

OLOS ANGELES DAILY NEWS | SERVING THE SAN FERNANDO VALLEY REGION

BARACK OBAMA — THE 44TH PRESIDENT

A NEW DAY

WEDNESDAY JANUARY 21, 2009

mX

SPECIAL COMMEMORATIVE EDITION

" *To all the other peoples and governments who are watching today, from the grandest capitals to the small village where my father was born: know that America is a friend of each nation and every man, woman and child who seeks a future of peace and dignity, and we are ready to lead once more.* "

INSIDE ★ THE SPEECH ★ THE PARADE ★ THE REACTION

120

Chicago Tribune

TUESDAY, JANUARY 20, 2009 | The Midwest's largest reporting team | 24 hours at chicagotribune.com

AN AMERICAN MOMENT

121

122

היום מתחיל עידן אובמה

Good Luck

4 מיליון משתתפים ★ 42 אלף מאבטחים ★ עשר מסיבות ★ כך תיראה ההשבעה
של הנשיא השחור הראשון בתולדות אמריקה ★ אורלי אזולאי, עמ' 2 ורב"24 שעות"

התשובי הטרי שנפצע
אנושות חוזר לחיים

התרגשות גדולה בבית החולים: סג"מ אהרן קרוב
שב להכרה ומסוגל לתקשר ● ראובן וייס, עמ' 6

בחירות 2009 עוד 3 שבועות בדיוק

סערה בליכוד: הח"כים
נעלמו משלטי החוצות

123

Wednesday
January 21, 2009
Volume 4, No. 197

Newton Citizen

Covington, Georgia
50 Cents

HOPE MEETS HISTORY

Obama takes spot as first black president

By JENNIFER LOVEN
The Associated Press

WASHINGTON — Before a jubilant crowd of more than a million, Barack Hussein Obama claimed his place in history as America's first black president, summoning a dispirited nation to unite in hope against the "gathering clouds and raging storms" of war and economic woe.

On an extraordinary day in the life of America, people of all colors and ages waited for hours Tuesday in frigid temperatures to witness a young black man with a foreign-sounding name take command of a nation founded by slaveholders. It was a scene watched in fascination by many millions — perhaps billions — around the world.

"We gather because we have chosen hope over fear, unity of purpose over conflict and discord," the nation's 44th president said.

The presidency passed to Democrat Obama from Republican George W. Bush at the stroke of noon, marking one of democracy's greatest gifts, the peaceful transfer of power.

But a stark transfer all the same. In one of the new administration's first acts, Obama ordered federal agencies to halt all pending regulations

•See Obama, Page 10A

Betty Bohler clasps an American flag and bows her head reverently as a prayer is given at President Barack Obama's inauguration Tuesday. About 50 seniors gathered at the Turner Lake Complex to view the ceremony.

Seniors celebrate inauguration

By CRYSTAL TATUM
Staff Reporter

COVINGTON — Local

Seniors spoke of how the moment, for them, signified the fulfillment of the dream of equality espoused by Dr. Mar

Esther
Williams/DC/USEPA/US
12/09/2008 12:50 PM

To Cheryl Williams/DC/USEPA/US@EPA, MaryE
Proctor/DC/USEPA/US@EPA, Inez
Powers/DC/USEPA/US@EPA

cc

bcc

Subject Fw: OBAMA THANKSGIVING

-FYI

Subject: FW: OBAMA THANKSGIVING

Subject: FW: OBAMA THANKSGIVING

CHICAGO - President-elect Barrack Obama and his wife <u>took their daughters</u> <u>to work</u> at a food bank on the day before Thanksgiving, saying <u>they wanted</u> <u>to show the girls the meaning of the holiday, especially when so many</u> <u>people are struggling.</u>

Ten-year-old Malia and 7-year-old Sasha joined their parents to shake hands and give holiday wishes to hundreds of people who had been lined up for hours at the food bank on Chicago 's south side.

Sasha wore a pink stocking hat over her pigtails and Malia had on a purple striped hat as the family handed out wrapped chickens to the needy in the chilly outdoor courtyard. Those seeking food on Wednesday at St. Columbanus also received boxes with potatoes, oranges, fresh bread, peanut butter, canned goods, oatmeal, spaghetti and coffee.

The president-elect, dressed casually in a leather jacket, black scarf and khaki pants, was in a jovial mood, calling out "happy thanksgiving" and telling everyone "you can call me Barack."

128

He told reporters that <u>he wants the girls "to learn the importance of how</u> <u>fortunate they are, and to make sure they're giving back."</u>
The soon-to-be first lady said the Obamas wanted to give their children "an understanding of what giving and Thanksgiving is all about."

"I just wanted to come by and wish everybody a happy Thanksgiving," he said. He then asked the children what they would be eating for Thanksgiving dinner.

So lets recap.

130

The Obama family's activities in the courtyard quickly drew the attention of schoolchildren whose windows overlooked the courtyard. They put up a sign against the glass that read: "We love our prez" and screamed when the president-elect waved to them.

Obama then turned to his wife and suggested they go visit the kids. Secret Service agents, looking surprised, disappeared inside the building to accommodate his request.
Minutes later, hundreds of children were brought down to the school auditorium, and Obama loped onstage as they screamed and cheered.

He took his kids to work in the cold...? Instead of getting someone to line up and dish the gifts? Instead of telling them 'You are kids of a VIP. Therefore there are things that you can't do.
To show the kids that people are suffering? Yes, that people are suffering? They have to live understanding the importance of giving back to the community.
Let us learn from this great family... and for those who have children, this is a wonderful example of raising our kids.
Peace out!

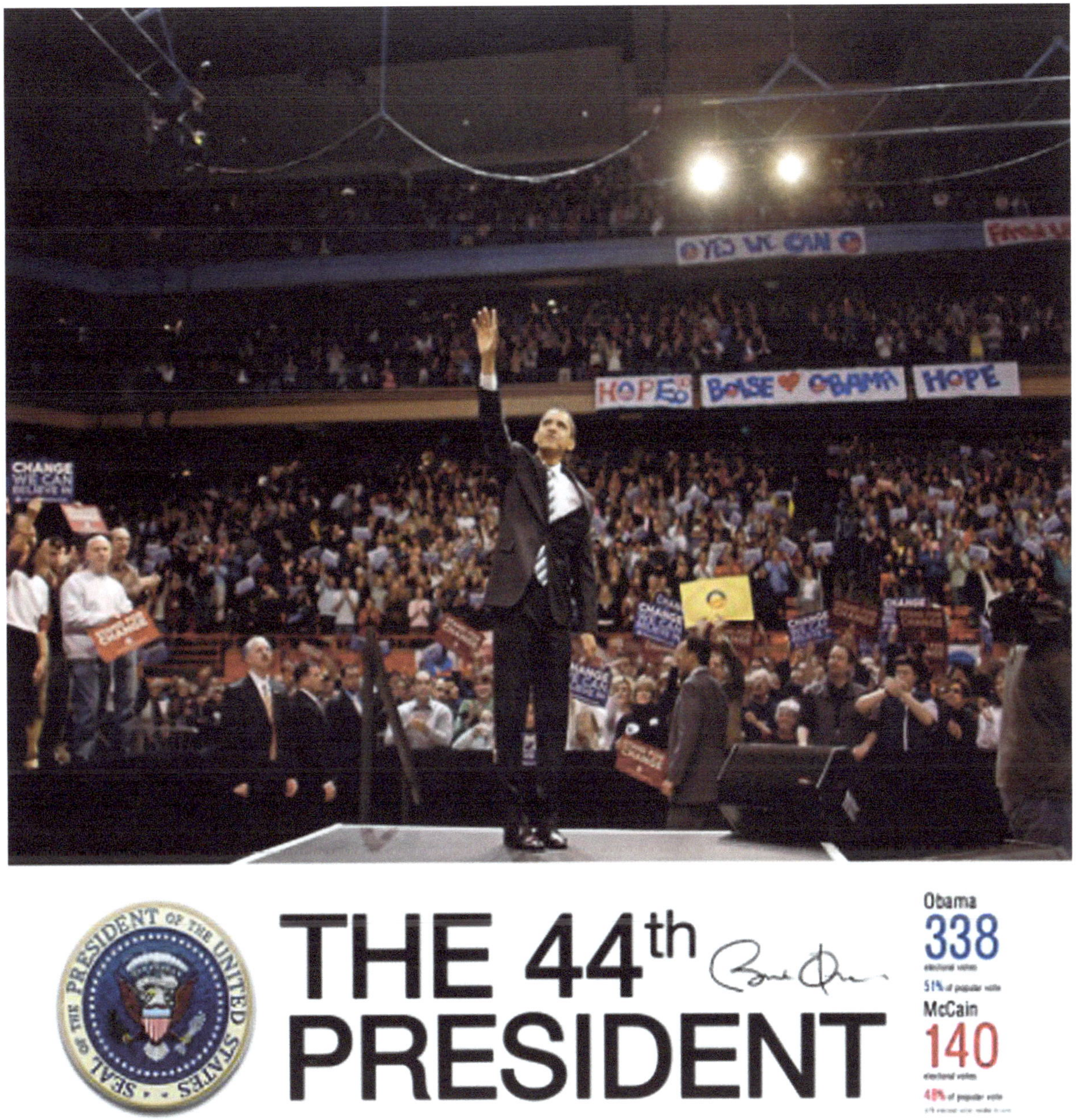

THE 44th
PRESIDENT

Obama
338
electoral votes
51% of popular vote

McCain
140
electoral votes
48% of popular vote

March 2009

S	M	T	W	T	F	S
1	2	3	4	5	6	7
8	9	10	11	12	13	14
15	16	17	18	19	20	21
22	23	24	25	26	27	28

April 2009

135

May 2009

S	M	T	W	T	F	S
					1	2
3	4	5	6	7	8	9
10	11	12	13	14	15	16<>
17	18	19	20	21	22	23
24	25	26	27	28	29	30
31						

June 2009

S	M	T	W	T	F	S<>
	1	2	3	4	5	6<>
7	8	9	10	11	12	13<>
14	15	16	17	18	19	20
21	22	23	24		26	
28	29	30				

July 2009

138

August 2009

139

140

First Family

November 2009

"Free at last! Free at last! Thank God almighty, we're free at last . . !"

Change has come

December 2009

M	T	W	T	F	S
	2	3	4	5<>	
	9	10	11	12<>	
	16	17	18	19<>	
	23	24	25	26<>	
	30	31			

BEEN A LONG TIME COMING

144

150

De·ter·mi·na·tion
(di-ˌtər-mə-ˈnā-shən): firm or fixed intention to achieve a desired end.

153

154

156

157

160

172

181

184

197

 NEWS

FULL TRANSCRIPT: President Barack Obama's Inaugural Address

President Barack Obama delivers inaugural address from Washington, D.C.

By ABC News
January 21, 2009, 12:16 AM

Jan. 20, 2009 -- *Full transcript as prepared for delivery of President Barack Obama's inaugural remarks on Jan. 20, 2009, at the United States Capitol in Washington, D.C.*

My fellow citizens:

I stand here today humbled by the task before us, grateful for the trust you have bestowed, mindful of the sacrifices borne by our ancestors. I thank President Bush for his service to our nation, as well as the generosity and cooperation he has shown throughout this transition.

Forty-four Americans have now taken the presidential oath. The words have been spoken during rising tides of prosperity and the still waters of peace. Yet, every so often the oath is taken amidst gathering clouds and raging storms. At these moments, America has carried on not simply because of the skill or vision of those in high office, but because We the People have remained faithful to the ideals of our forbearers, and true to our founding documents.

So it has been. So it must be with this generation of Americans.

That we are in the midst of crisis is now well understood. Our nation is at war, against a far-reaching network of violence and hatred. Our economy is badly weakened, a consequence of greed and irresponsibility on the part of some, but also our collective failure to make hard choices and prepare the nation for a new age. Homes have been lost; jobs shed; businesses shuttered. Our health care is too costly; our schools fail too many; and each day brings further evidence that the ways we use energy strengthen our adversaries and threaten our planet.

These are the indicators of crisis, subject to data and statistics. Less measurable but no less profound is a sapping of confidence across our land - a nagging fear that America's decline is inevitable, and that the next generation must lower its sights.

Today I say to you that the challenges we face are real. They are serious and they are many.

They will not be met easily or in a short span of time. But know this, America - they will be met. On this day, we gather because we have chosen hope over fear, unity of purpose over conflict and discord.

On this day, we come to proclaim an end to the petty grievances and false promises, the recriminations and worn out dogmas, that for far too long have strangled our politics.

We remain a young nation, but in the words of Scripture, the time has come to set aside childish things. The time has come to reaffirm our enduring spirit; to choose our better history; to carry forward that precious gift, that noble idea, passed on from generation to generation: the God-given promise that all are equal, all are free, and all deserve a chance to pursue their full measure of happiness.

In reaffirming the greatness of our nation, we understand that greatness is never a given. It must be earned. Our journey has never been one of short-cuts or settling for less. It has not been the path for the faint-hearted - for those who prefer leisure over work, or seek only the pleasures of riches and fame. Rather, it has been the risk-takers, the doers, the makers of things - some celebrated but more often men and women obscure in their labor, who have carried us up the long, rugged path towards prosperity and freedom.

For us, they packed up their few worldly possessions and traveled across oceans in search of a new life.

For us, they toiled in sweatshops and settled the West; endured the lash of the whip and plowed the hard earth.

For us, they fought and died, in places like Concord and Gettysburg; Normandy and Khe Sahn. Time and again these men and women struggled and sacrificed and worked till their hands were raw so that we might live a better life. They saw America as bigger than the sum of our individual ambitions; greater than all the differences of birth or wealth or faction.

This is the journey we continue today. We remain the most prosperous, powerful nation on Earth. Our workers are no less productive than when this crisis began. Our minds are no less inventive, our goods and services no less needed than they were last week or last month or last year. Our capacity remains undiminished. But our time of standing pat, of protecting narrow interests and putting off unpleasant decisions - that time has surely passed. Starting today, we must pick ourselves up, dust ourselves off, and begin again the work of remaking America.

For everywhere we look, there is work to be done. The state of the economy calls for action, bold and swift, and we will act - not only to create new jobs, but to lay a new foundation for growth. We will build the roads and bridges, the electric grids and digital lines that feed our commerce and bind us together. We will restore science to its rightful place, and wield technology's wonders to raise health care's quality and lower its cost. We will harness the sun and the winds and the soil to fuel our cars and run our factories. And we will transform our schools and colleges and universities to meet the demands of a new age. All this we can do. And all this we will do.

Now, there are some who question the scale of our ambitions - who suggest that our system cannot tolerate too many big plans. Their memories are short. For they have forgotten what this country has already done; what free men and women can achieve when imagination is joined to common purpose, and necessity to courage.

What the cynics fail to understand is that the ground has shifted beneath them - that the stale political arguments that have consumed us for so long no longer apply. The question we ask today is not whether our government is too big or too small, but whether it works - whether it helps families find jobs at a decent wage, care they can afford, a retirement that is dignified. Where the answer is yes, we intend to move forward. Where the answer is no, programs will end. And those of us who manage the public's dollars will be held to account - to spend wisely, reform bad habits, and do our business in the light of day - because only then can we restore the vital trust between a people and their government.

Nor is the question before us whether the market is a force for good or ill. Its power to generate wealth and expand freedom is unmatched, but this crisis has reminded us that without a watchful eye, the market can spin out of control - and that a nation cannot prosper long when it favors only the prosperous. The success of our economy has always depended not just on the size of our Gross Domestic Product, but on the reach of our prosperity; on our ability to extend opportunity to every willing heart - not out of charity, but because it is the surest route to our common good.

As for our common defense, we reject as false the choice between our safety and our ideals. Our Founding Fathers, faced with perils we can scarcely imagine, drafted a charter to assure the rule of law and the rights of man, a charter expanded by the blood of generations. Those ideals still light the world, and we will not give them up for expedience's sake. And so to all other peoples and governments who are watching today, from the grandest capitals to the small village where my father was born: know that America is a friend of each nation and every man, woman, and child who seeks a future of peace and dignity, and that we are ready to lead once more.

Recall that earlier generations faced down fascism and communism not just with missiles and tanks, but with sturdy alliances and enduring convictions. They understood that our power alone cannot protect us, nor does it entitle us to do as we please. Instead, they knew that our power grows through its prudent use; our security emanates from the justness of our cause, the force of our example, the tempering qualities of humility and restraint.

We are the keepers of this legacy. Guided by these principles once more, we can meet those new threats that demand even greater effort - even greater cooperation and understanding between nations. We will begin to responsibly leave Iraq to its people, and forge a hard-earned peace in Afghanistan. With old friends and former foes, we will work tirelessly to lessen the nuclear threat, and roll back the specter of a warming planet. We will not apologize for our way of life, nor will we waver in its defense, and for those who seek to advance their aims by inducing terror and slaughtering innocents, we say to you now that our spirit is stronger and cannot be broken; you cannot outlast us, and we will defeat you.

For we know that our patchwork heritage is a strength, not a weakness. We are a nation of Christians and Muslims, Jews and Hindus - and non-believers. We are shaped by every language and culture, drawn from every end of this Earth; and because we have tasted the bitter swill of civil war and segregation, and emerged from that dark chapter stronger and more united, we cannot help but believe that the old hatreds shall someday pass; that the lines of tribe shall soon dissolve; that as the world grows smaller, our common humanity shall reveal itself; and that America must play its role in ushering in a new era of peace.

To the Muslim world, we seek a new way forward, based on mutual interest and mutual respect.

To those leaders around the globe who seek to sow conflict, or blame their society's ills on the West - know that your people will judge you on what you can build, not what you destroy. To those who cling to power through corruption and deceit and the silencing of dissent, know that you are on the wrong side of history; but that we will extend a hand if you are willing to unclench your fist.

To the people of poor nations, we pledge to work alongside you to make your farms flourish and let clean waters flow; to nourish starved bodies and feed hungry minds. And to those nations like ours that enjoy relative plenty, we say we can no longer afford indifference to suffering outside our borders; nor can we consume the world's resources without regard to effect. For the world has changed, and we must change with it.

As we consider the road that unfolds before us, we remember with humble gratitude those brave Americans who, at this very hour, patrol far-off deserts and distant mountains. They have something to tell us today, just as the fallen heroes who lie in Arlington whisper through the ages.

We honor them not only because they are guardians of our liberty, but because they embody the spirit of service; a willingness to find meaning in something greater than themselves. And yet, at this moment - a moment that will define a generation - it is precisely this spirit that must inhabit us all.

For as much as government can do and must do, it is ultimately the faith and determination of the American people upon which this nation relies. It is the kindness to take in a stranger when the levees break, the selflessness of workers who would rather cut their hours than see a friend lose their job which sees us through our darkest hours. It is the firefighter's courage to storm a stairway filled with smoke, but also a parent's willingness to nurture a child, that finally decides our fate.

Our challenges may be new. The instruments with which we meet them may be new. But those values upon which our success depends - hard work and honesty, courage and fair play, tolerance and curiosity, loyalty and patriotism - these things are old. These things are true. They have been the quiet force of progress throughout our history. What is demanded then is a return to these truths. What is required of us now is a new era of responsibility - a recognition, on the part of every American, that we have duties to ourselves, our nation, and the world, duties that we do not grudgingly accept but rather seize gladly, firm in the knowledge that there is nothing so satisfying to the spirit, so defining of our character, than giving our all to a difficult task.

This is the price and the promise of citizenship.

This is the source of our confidence - the knowledge that God calls on us to shape an uncertain destiny.

This is the meaning of our liberty and our creed - why men and women and children of every race and every faith can join in celebration across this magnificent mall, and why a man whose father less than sixty years ago might not have been served at a local restaurant can now stand before you to take a most sacred oath.

So let us mark this day with remembrance, of who we are and how far we have traveled. In the year of America's birth, in the coldest of months, a small band of patriots huddled by dying campfires on the shores of an icy river. The capital was abandoned. The enemy was advancing. The snow was stained with blood. At a moment when the outcome of our revolution was most in doubt, the father of our nation ordered these words be read to the people:

"Let it be told to the future world...that in the depth of winter, when nothing but hope and virtue could survive...that the city and the country, alarmed at one common danger, came forth to meet [it]."

America. In the face of our common dangers, in this winter of our hardship, let us remember these timeless words. With hope and virtue, let us brave once more the icy currents, and endure what storms may come. Let it be said by our children's children that when we were tested we refused to let this journey end, that we did not turn back nor did we falter; and with eyes fixed on the horizon and God's grace upon us, we carried forth that great gift of freedom and delivered it safely to future generations.

Sign In | Register Now

boston.com

Local Search   Site Search

| HOME | TODAY'S GLOBE | NEWS | BUSINESS | SPORTS | LIFESTYLE | A&E | THINGS TO DO | TF |

News stories in photographs

FAQ   About | RSS

By Alan Taylor

(Use

1405 comments   January 21, 2009

Yahoo! Buzz

ShareThis

The Inauguration of President Barack Obama

Yesterday was a historic day. On January 20th, 2009, Barack H. Obama was swo
States of America - the first African-American ever to hold the office of U.S. Com
well over one million attendees in chilly Washington D.C., and by many millions 1
Internet. Collected here are photographs of the event, the participants, and some

photos total)

The Capitol is illuminated in the early morning hours before the inauguration of Barack Obama as the 44th President of the United States of America January 20, 2009 in Washington, DC. (David McNew/Getty Images)

2 People gather to watch US President Barack Obama's sworn in as the 44th US president by Supreme Court Chief Justice John Roberts in front of the US Capitol in Washington, DC on January 20, 2009. (JEWEL SAMAD/AFP/Getty Images) #

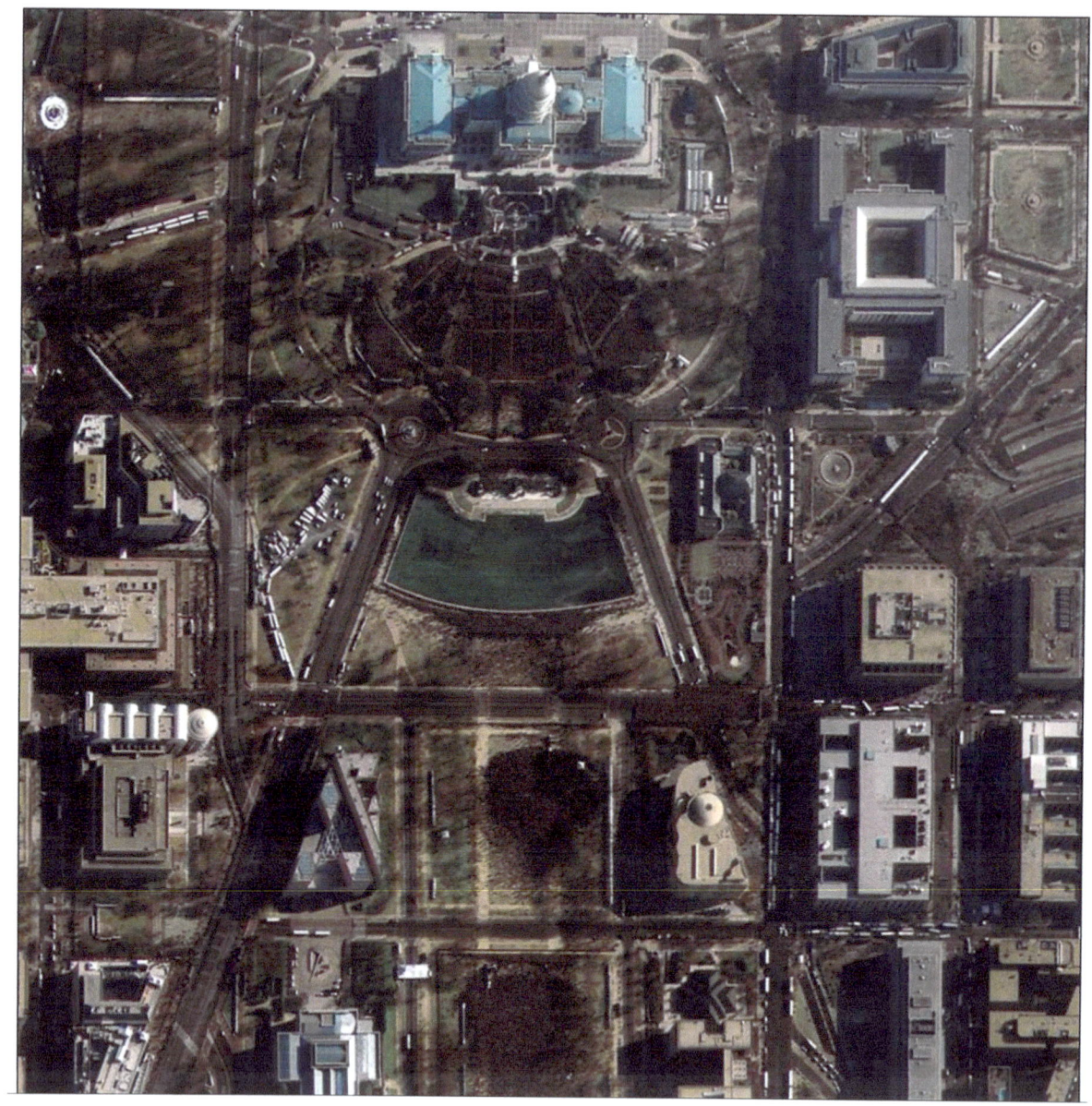

3 This image provided by GeoEye Satellite Image shows Washington D.C.'s National Mall and the United States Capitol (top), in Washington D.C. on Tuesday, Jan. 20, 2009 taken at 11:19AM EDT during the inauguration of President Barack Obama. The image, taken through high, wispy white clouds, shows the masses of people between the Capitol and the Washington Monument. (AP Photo/GeoEye Satellite Image) #

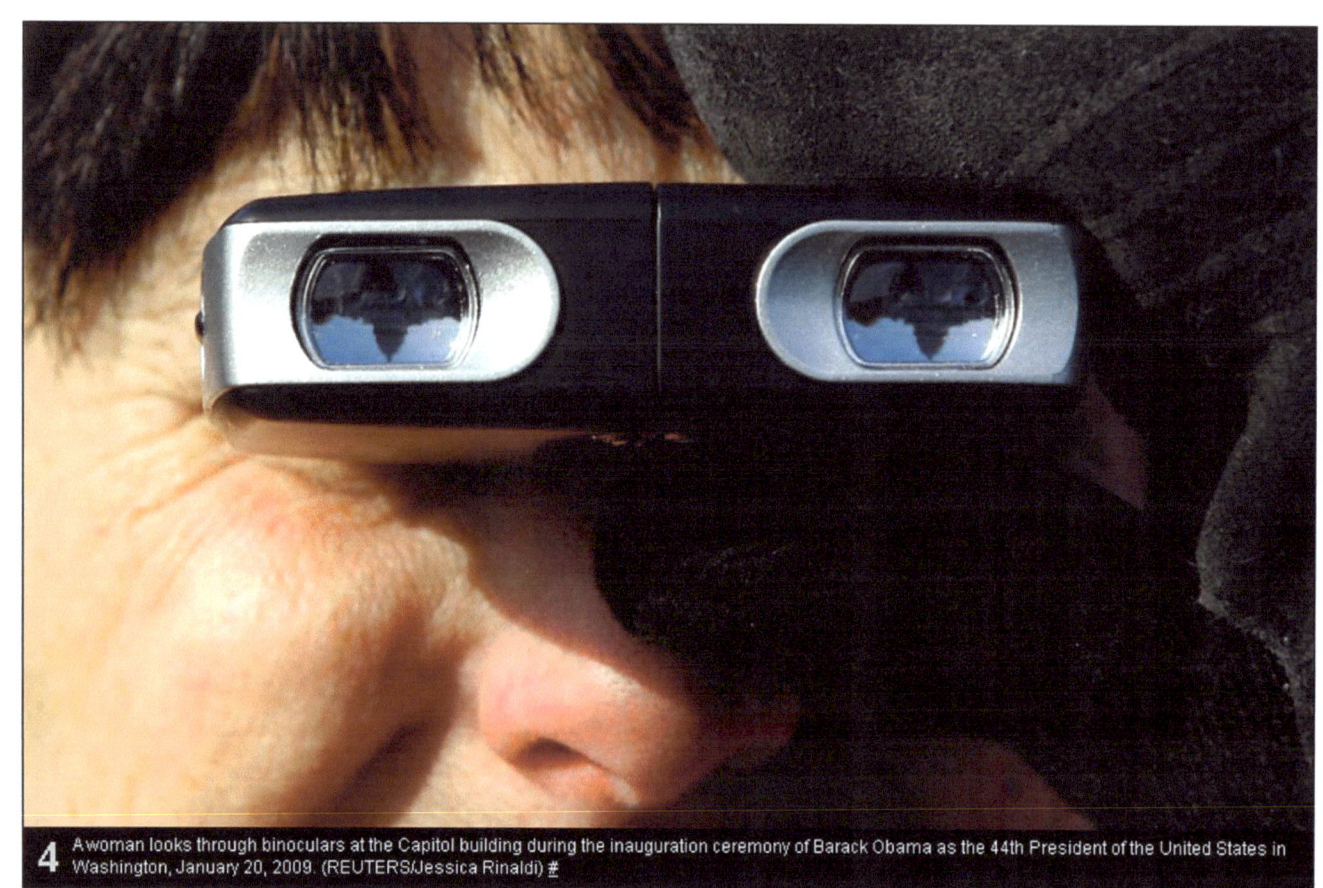

4 A woman looks through binoculars at the Capitol building during the inauguration ceremony of Barack Obama as the 44th President of the United States in Washington, January 20, 2009. (REUTERS/Jessica Rinaldi) #

214

5 President-elect Barack Obama takes the oath of office from Chief Justice John Roberts to become the 44th President of the United States on Capitol Hill in Washington, Tuesday, Jan. 20, 2009. (AP Photo/Susan Walsh) #

6 Barack H. Obama is sworn in as the 44th president of the United States as his wife Michelle Obama holds the Bible and their daughters Malia Obama and Sasha Obama look on, on the West Front of the Capitol January 20, 2009 in Washington, DC. (Chuck Kennedy-Pool/Getty Images) #

7 President Barack Obama delivers his inaugural address after being sworn in by Chief Justice John Roberts as the 44th president of the United States as the 44th President of the United States of America at the Capitol January 20, 2009 in Washington, DC. (Jim Bourg-Pool/Getty Images) #

8 People cheer at the Washington Monument during the inauguration ceremony of U.S. President Barack Obama in Washington January 20, 2009. (REUTERS/Mark Blinch) #

9 Spectators in Times Square watch President Barack Obama take the oath of office during his inauguration Tuesday, Jan. 20, 2009 in New York. (AP Photo/Jason DeCrow) #

10 Residents of Kibera, one of the poorest quarters in Nairobi gather to watch the inauguration ceremony of US President Barack Obama in Nairobi on January 20, 2009. (YASUYOSHI CHIBA/AFP/Getty Images) #

220

11 People watch a big television screen broadcasting Barack Obama being sworn in as the 44th President of the United States of America on the West Front of the Capitol in Washington, Tuesday, Jan. 20, 2009 during a ceremony at the Paris town hall in Paris, France. (AP Photo/Jacques Brinon) #

12 Iraqis gather to watch televised coverage of the inauguration of U.S. President Barack Obama at a cafe in the Shiite stronghold of Sadr City in Baghdad, Iraq on Tuesday, Jan. 20, 2009. (AP Photo/Karim Kadim) #

13 U.S. soldiers watch the U.S. presidential inauguration via a webcast from Combat Outpost Keating in eastern Afghanistan January 20, 2009. (REUTERS/Bob Strong (AFGHANISTAN) #

14 Cecilia Perez, center, watches the inauguration of U.S. President Barack Obama with Oscar Rodriguez at her taco stand in Mexico City, Jan. 20, 2009. (AP Photo/Gregory Bull) #

224

15 Villagers of Nyang'oma Kogelo, the Kenyan village where 44th US President Barack Obama's father was born, react as they watch on a giant screen inauguration ceremony of US President Barack Obama, on January 20, 2009. Thousands of people from around and beyond Kogelo, including foreign tourists gathered at Nyang'oma village to celebrate the inauguration of Obama. (TONY KARUMBA/AFP/Getty Images) #

16 Shoppers watch the inauguration of President Barack Obama at the Best Buy Store at the Mall of America in Bloomington, Minn., Tuesday, Jan. 20, 2009. (AP Photo/Jim Mone) #

17 People gather for the inauguration of Barack Obama as the 44th President of the United States of America on the National Mall January 20, 2009 in Washington, DC. (Mario Tama/Getty Images) #

18 The Rev. Joseph Lowery gives the benediction during the inauguration of Barack Obama as the 44th President of the United States of America on the West Front of the Capitol January 20, 2009 in Washington, DC. (Alex Wong/Getty Images) #

19 US Army Command Sgt. Maj. Julia Kelley, left, of the 229th Brigade Support Battalion, 2nd Heavy Brigade Combat Team, 1st Infantry Division, weeps as she watches the inauguration of US President Barack Obama at Camp Liberty in Baghdad, Iraq, Tuesday, Jan. 20, 2009. #

20 People attend the inauguration of Barack Obama as the 44th president of the United States on the National Mall January 20, 2009 in Washington, DC. (Mario Tama/Getty Images) #

21 U.S. President Barack H. Obama greets guests after he is sworn in as the 44th president of the United States on the West Front of the Capitol January 20, 2009 in Washington, DC. (J. Scott Applewhite-Pool/Getty Images) #

22 Keith Hart, center, a Vietnam Army veteran, cheers as he watches Barack Obama be inaugurated as president, on television with other patrons of the Oxford Bar in Missoula, Mt., one of the oldest bars in Montana, on Tuesday, Jan. 20, 2009. (AP Photo/Michael Albans) #

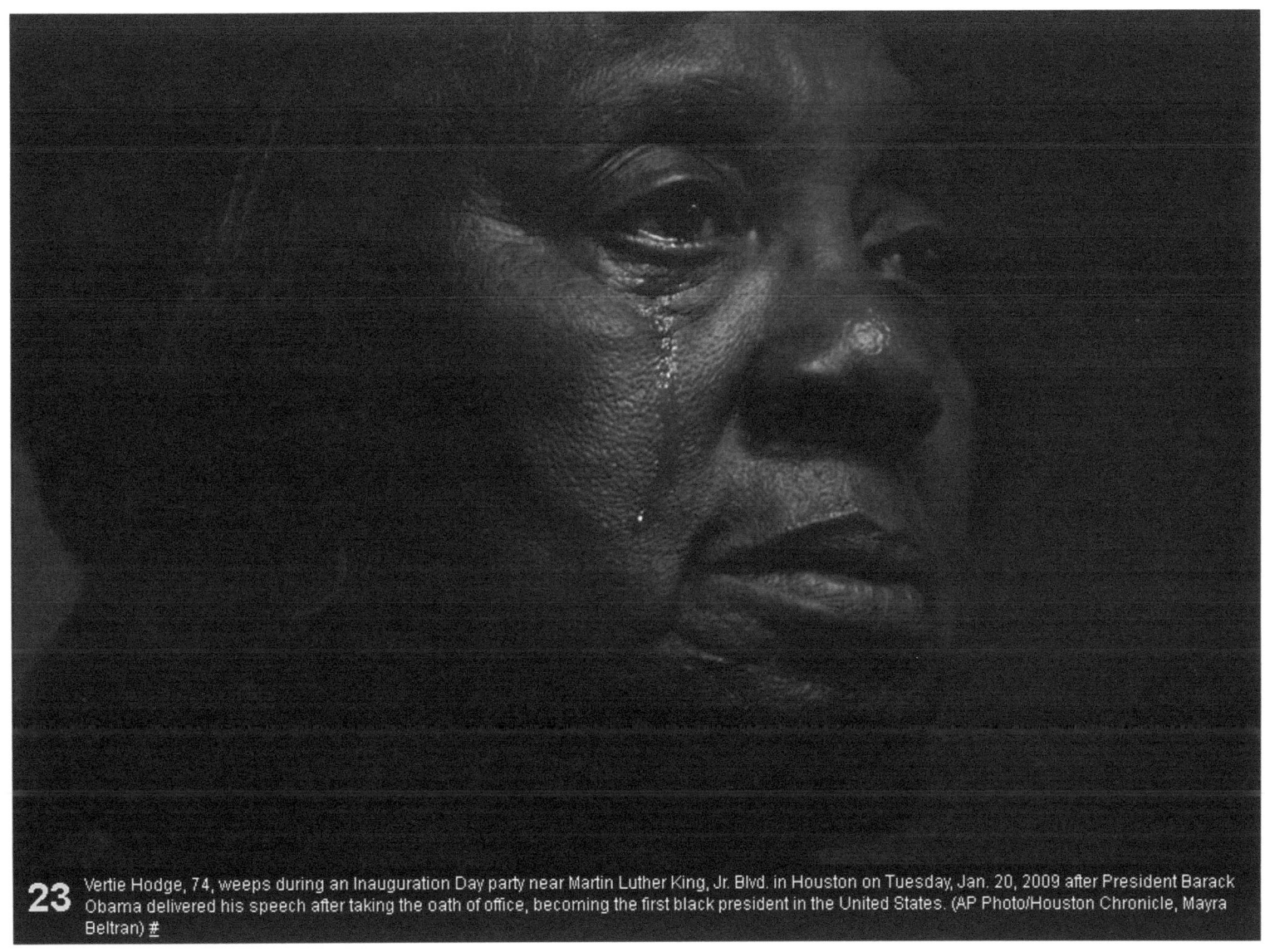

23 Vertie Hodge, 74, weeps during an Inauguration Day party near Martin Luther King, Jr. Blvd. in Houston on Tuesday, Jan. 20, 2009 after President Barack Obama delivered his speech after taking the oath of office, becoming the first black president in the United States. (AP Photo/Houston Chronicle, Mayra Beltran) #

24 Members of a US Navy Honor Guard stand at attention as US President Barack Obama and first lady Michelle Obama arrive at the Presidential Reviewing Stand during the Inaugural Parade January 20, 2009 in Washington, DC. (Chip Somodevilla/Getty Images) #

25 President Barack Obama and his wife Michelle stand with former US president George W. Bush and Laura Bush on the steps of the US Capitol following the inaugural ceremony for Obama as 44th US president in Washington on January 20, 2009. (EMMANUEL DUNAND/AFP/Getty Images) #

26 Former President George W. Bush and Laura Bush wave as they board a Marine helicopter at the Capitol in Washington after Barack Obama was sworn in as the 44th president of the United States, Tuesday, Jan. 20, 2009. (AP Photo/Charles Dharapak) #

27 A Marine helicopter with former President George W. Bush on board departs from the East Front of the U.S. Capitol Tuesday, Jan. 20, 2009, in Washington, as President Barack Obama, first lady Michelle Obama, Vice President Joe Biden and his wife wave goodbye from the steps of the Capitol. (AP Photo/Tannen Maury, Pool) #

28 Former President George W. Bush looks out over the U.S. Capitol as his helicopter departs Washington, D.C. January 20, 2009, for Andrews Air Force Base following the inauguration ceremonies for President Barack Obama. (ERIC DRAPER/AFP/Getty Images) #

29 Mujo Bota and Alamasa Bota, Bosnian Muslims, watch a TV broadcast of the inauguration of U.S. President Barack Obama with their grandson Ajdin Bota, 10, in the village of Dejicici, near Sarajevo, Bosnia Herzegovina on Tuesday Jan. 20, 2009. (AP Photo/Amel Emric) #

30 Students of the Crested Butte Community School, in Crested Butte Colo. sit on the floor in the main hallway of the school and applaud the inaugural address of President Barack Obama while watching the presidential inauguration in Washington, Tuesday, Jan., 20, 2009. (AP Photo/Nathan Bilow) #

31 Afghan men watch a television broadcast showing the inauguration of Barack Obama as the 44th president of the United States, at a restaurant in Kabul, Afghanistan, Tuesday, Jan 20, 2009. (AP Photo/Ahmad Masoud) #

32 Kenyans who gathered at the grounds of the University of Nairobi to watch in giant screens the inauguration ceremony where Obama was sworn in as the 44th President of the United States of America celebrate the ocassion on January 20, 2008. Barrack Obama's father was born in Kenya. #

242

33 40 years after their silent protest at the 1968 Olympics, Gold Medalist Tommie Smith hugs Bronze Medalist John Carlos, and their wives Delois Smith and Charlene Carlos after Barack Obama is officially sworn in as the President of the United States. Photo taken in the Smith room at the Sheraton Boston in Boston, MA. (Boston Globe/Stan Grossfeld) #

34 U.S. President Barack Obama with his wife Michelle at the inaugural luncheon after he was sworn in as the 44th President of the United States in Washington, January 20, 2009. (REUTERS/Yuri Gripas) #

35 U.S. President Barack Obama talks with U.S. Sen. John McCain after arriving at the luncheon at Statuary Hall the luncheon at Statuary Hall in the U.S. Capitol on January 20, 2009 in Washington, DC. (Amanda Rivkin-Pool/Getty Images) #

36 President Barack Obama signs his first act as president, a proclamation declaring a national day of renewal and reconciliation and calling on Americans to serve one another, after being sworn in as the 44th President of the United States during the inaugural ceremony in Washington Tuesday, Jan. 20, 2009. (AP Photo/Molly Riley, Pool) #

37 A South Korean man reads a newspaper reporting on U.S. President Barack Obama's Inauguration on the subway in Seoul, South Korea, Wednesday, Jan. 21, 2009. (AP Photo/ Lee Jin-man) #

38 Pakistani Christian children hold portraits of U.S. President-elect Barack Obama during a prayers ceremony for global peace in Islamabad, Pakistan on Tuesday, Jan. 20, 2009. (AP Photo) #

39 People wave American flags at the inauguration of Barack Obama as the 44th president of the United States on the National Mall January 20, 2009 in Washington, DC. (Mario Tama/Getty Images) #

40 U.S. President Barack Obama and first lady Michelle Obama walk in the inaugural parade following his inauguration as the 44th President of the United States of America on January 20, 2009 in Washington, D.C. (Doug Mills-Pool/Getty Images) #

41 Sasha Obama waves through the limousine window as she and her sister Malia leave Capitol Hill in Washington, Tuesday, Jan. 20, 2009. (AP Photo/Susan Walsh) #

42 U.S. Navy Chief Petty Officer Bill Mesta replaces an official picture of outgoing President George W. Bush with that of newly-sworn-in U.S. President Barack Obama, in the lobby of the headquarters of the U.S. Naval Base January 20, 2009 in Guantanamo Bay, Cuba. (Brennan Linsley-Pool/Getty Images) #

43 President Barack Obama and First Lady Michelle Obama attend the Neighborhood Inaugural Ball at the Washington Convention Center on January 20, 2009 in Washington, DC. (Photo by Chip Somodevilla/Getty Images) #

44 Guests at the "Biden Home States Ball" record the moment as President Barack Obama and first lady Michelle Obama dance at the Washington Convention Center in the nation's capital, Tuesday, Jan. 20, 2009. (AP Photo/J. Scott Applewhite) #

45 Vice President Joe Biden and his wife Jill dance during the Commander in Chief's Ball at the National Building Museum in Washington January 20 2009 . (TIMOTHY A. CLARY/AFP/Getty Images) #

46 U.S. President Barack Obama and first lady Michelle Obama dance their first dance at the Neighborhood Inaugural Ball in Washington January 20, 2009. (REUTERS/Jason Reed) #

47 People watching President Barack Obama's inauguration via television raise a toast to the nation's new president at Brooklyn's Fort Greene Senior Action Center in New York, Tuesday, Jan. 20, 2009. (AP Photo/Kathy Willens) #

270

271

274

275

283

289

294

President
Barack Obama
November 4th, 2008

295

297